Thomas Hitchcock

Unhappy Loves

of men of genius

Thomas Hitchcock

Unhappy Loves
of men of genius

ISBN/EAN: 9783741101410

Manufactured in Europe, USA, Canada, Australia, Japa

Cover: Foto ©Andreas Hilbeck / pixelio.de

Manufactured and distributed by brebook publishing software (www.brebook.com)

Thomas Hitchcock

Unhappy Loves

UNHAPPY LOVES

OF

MEN OF GENIUS

BY

THOMAS HITCHCOCK

NEW YORK
HARPER & BROTHERS, FRANKLIN SQUARE
1891

PREFACE.

IN this volume the author has collected some sketches heretofore published separately of experiences in love by men of genius which have not had happy conclusions. Except in the case of Cavour and the Unknown, the leading incidents narrated have long been familiar to the public, and it is only for their new arrangement and treatment that any pretence to originality is made.

The feature of these affairs which has most interested the author is that the women concerned in them were, equally with the men, distinguished by their gifts and their accomplishments. Madame Necker was one of the intellectual queens of her day. Mrs. Thrale possessed uncommon literary and conversational talent. Charlotte von Stein was Goethe's companion in his studies and in his literary work, as well as in his leisure hours. Aloysia Weber was a musical artist of the highest order; the few letters remaining of Cavour's Unknown prove that she possessed a highly poetical nature, while Mrs. Carlyle's wit and acquirements were, from her earliest years, the admiration of all who knew her. Some of these women had beauty, but it was their mental charms and not their beauty which captivated their lovers.

The sketches, therefore, apart from the common human interest which they possess, will serve as materials for the study of love in its more refined and elevated form. And if any one who takes up this book is disposed to smile at its contents, let him remember these words of Dr. Johnson: "We must not ridicule a passion which he who never felt never was happy; and he who laughs at never deserves to feel—a passion which has caused the change of empires and the loss of worlds—a passion which has inspired heroism and subdued avarice."

NEW YORK, *May*, 1891.

CONTENTS.

	PAGE

GIBBON AND MADAME NECKER............   1

Gibbon at Lausanne, 2.—His own story of his love, 4.—Madame Necker's girlhood, 7.—Her personal appearance, 8.—Gibbon's first letters, 11. — His lukewarm passion, 13. — His return to England, 15. — His farewell letter, 16.—Her expostulations, 18.—Rousseau's opinion of Gibbon, 21. — The final rupture, 23.—Madame Necker's marriage, 24. — Her social success, 25. — Monsieur Necker, 29.—Gibbon's character, 31.—The "Decline and Fall," 32.—Correspondence renewed, 35.—A regretful letter, 37.—Matrimonial longings, 39. — Lady Elizabeth Foster, 41.—An undying friendship, 42.

DR. JOHNSON AND MRS. THRALE..   45

Boswell's slanders, 47.—Piozzi, 49.—Doctor Collier, 51.—Mrs. Thrale's attractions, 52.—Johnson's repulsiveness, 54. — Conversational ability, 57.—Fascination for women,

58.—Appreciation of beauty, 60.—Delicacy of feeling, 62.—Thrale's coarseness, 65.—Johnson's love, 67.—Bitter disappointment, 69.—Talk with Madame d'Arblay, 71.—A brutal letter, 72.—Love turned to hatred, 75.

GOETHE AND CHARLOTTE VON STEIN........ 77

Charlotte's character, 80.—Unhappy childhood, 81.—Goethe's beauty, 83.—Numerous love affairs, 85.—A new experience, 86.—Charlotte's fascinations, 89.—Letter-writing, 91.—Unromantic topics, 93.—Charlotte's piety, 95.—A passionate outburst, 97.—A despairing appeal, 99.—Wild longing, 101.—A peaceful record, 103.—Ecstasy, 105.—A lover's quarrel, 107.—Musical illustrations, 109.—Quiet happiness, 111.—Letters in French, 112.—Flight to Italy, 114.—Opinion of Weimar, 117.—A new theory, 119.—What Goethe expected, 121.—Last words of love, 123.—Christiane Vulpius, 125.—End of the romance, 127.—Resentment and reconciliation, 129.

MOZART AND ALOYSIA WEBER.............. 131

Mozart's character, 132.—Romantic ideas, 134.—Personal appearance, 137.—Mannheim, 139.—Aloysia's talent, 141.—Mozart's admiration, 143.—Planning a tour, 145.—Musical ambition, 147.—Paternal remonstrances, 149.—Filial submission, 150.—A sorrowful parting, 153.—Aloysia's inconstancy, 154.—Wonderful voice, 157.—Tardy regret, 159.

CONTENTS.

CAVOUR AND THE UNKNOWN............... 161
   Intellectual sympathy, 163.—A long separation, 165.—An ecstatic meeting, 167.—Vows of fidelity, 169.—An epistolary outpour, 170.—Religious sentiments, 173.—Disinterested love, 175.—Patient submission, 177.—A pathetic farewell, 179.—A lonely life, 181.

IRVING AND MRS. CARLYLE............... 183
   Mrs. Carlyle as a girl, 185.—Precocious talent, 187.—Irving's personal beauty, 189.—Bodily and mental vigor, 191.—Teacher and pupil, 193.—A thoughtless engagement, 195.—Dawning love, 197.—Intercourse with Carlyle, 199.—Irving's farewell, 200.—Career in London, 203.—Carlyle as a lover, 205.—Intellectual mastery, 207.—Unhappy married life, 209.—Irving's last visits, 211.

ILLUSTRATIONS.

Drawn expressly for this work by H. D. Nichols.

I. MADAME NECKER (after an old print).. *Frontispiece.*
II. EDWARD GIBBON (after the portrait by Sir Joshua Reynolds)..... *Facing page* 1
III. DR. SAMUEL JOHNSON (after the portrait by Sir Joshua Reynolds painted in 1773)................... *Facing page* 45
IV. MRS. THRALE (after the figure in "The Lady's Last Stake," for which she sat as model, painted by William Hogarth in 1756)................. *Facing page* 50
V. GOETHE (after the portrait painted by May in 1779)............ *Facing page* 77
VI. CHARLOTTE VON STEIN (after a sketch made by herself in 1790).. *Facing page* 80
VII. CHRISTIANE VULPIUS, Goethe's wife (after a crayon portrait taken in 1800)................... *Facing page* 126
VIII. MOZART (from the family group painted by Della Croce in 1780)... *Facing page* 131

ILLUSTRATIONS.

IX. COUNT CAVOUR (after a photograph from life)....................*Facing page* 161

X. JANE WELSH CARLYLE (after a miniature in the possession of Mr. Froude)..
Facing page 183

XI. EDWARD IRVING (after the portrait prefixed to Mrs. Oliphant's biography)....
Facing page 190

XII. THOMAS CARLYLE (after a portrait by Samuel Lawrence)........*Facing page* 200

EDWARD GIBBON.

GIBBON AND MADAME NECKER.

EDWARD GIBBON, the author of the "History of the Decline and Fall of the Roman Empire," was, so far as any record shows, only once seriously in love. If, like other men, he had occasional fancies for women, they ended as quickly as they began, and left no trace behind; but for Suzanne Curchod, afterwards Madame Necker, he experienced a passion which was as ardent as his nature would permit, and which, in a feeble, flickering way, endured till the end of his life.

In 1753, when Gibbon was a student at Oxford, and but sixteen years of age, he was induced by one of those caprices to which youth, and especially the youth of a genius, is liable, to become a Roman Catholic. His father, on learning of his apostasy, at once denounced it to the authorities of his college, which, as a matter of course, led to his expulsion, and then, both by way of punishment and for the purpose of reclaiming him from his error, he sent him to live at Lausanne, in Switzerland, as the pupil of a Protestant pastor in that town. The remedy was efficacious. In a few months Gibbon abjured his new faith as lightly as he had adopted it, and was formally received back into the Protestant communion. His tutor attributed this result to his polemic skill, but Gibbon himself asserts that it came from his own reading and reflection, which is probably true. Certainly, his subsequent career shows that he was not of the stuff out of which Roman Catholics are usually made, and that his Protestantism was rather negative than positive—more the want of all religious convictions than the possession of those he nominally professed.

This, however, was not the only important consequence of Gibbon's exile to Lausanne. It transformed his habits and his character, as well as his religion. Lamenting at first the loss of the comforts of his English home, and revolting at the strangeness of Swiss ways, he quickly adapted himself to his new conditions, and became, as he ever after continued to be, more of a foreigner than an Englishman. He learned in the course of two or three years to read, speak, and even to write French, as if it had been his mother tongue. So accustomed, indeed, was he to its use that his earliest production, at the age of twenty-four, "On the Study of Literature," was written in French; and when, at a later date, he undertook a history of the Swiss republics, he composed the first chapters of it in that language. Fortunately, the condemnation of this work, as far as it had proceeded, by the literary friends to whom he submitted it, prevented its completion, and the remonstrances of his fellow historian, David Hume, against the employment of French by an English author, induced him to adopt English when he came to write his monumental "Decline and Fall." But he kept his journal and made his literary notes always in French, and carried on in it his correspondence with his foreign friends, who complimented him upon the purity and the elegance of his style, and begged him to write in French altogether.

Being thus well equipped for Swiss society, Gibbon found his way into that of Lausanne, and there, at the commencement of his twenty-first year, he saw and loved Mademoiselle Curchod. His own account of the affair, as he gives it in the "Memoirs" written by himself thirty years afterwards, is as follows:

"I hesitate, from the apprehension of ridicule, when I approach the delicate subject of my early love. By this word I do not mean the polite attention, the gallantry, without hope or design, which has originated in the spirit of chivalry, and is interwoven with the texture of French manners. I understand by this passion the union of desire, friendship, and tenderness, which is inflamed by a single female, which prefers her to the rest of her sex, and which seeks her possession as the supreme or the sole happiness of our being. I need not blush at recollecting the object of my choice; and though my love was disappointed of success, I am rather proud that I was once capable of feeling such a pure and exalted sentiment. The personal attractions of Mademoiselle Susan Curchod were embellished by the virtues and talents of the mind. Her fortune was humble, but her family was respectable. Her mother, a native of France, had preferred her religion to her country. The profession of her father did not extinguish the moderation and philosophy of his temper, and he lived content with a small salary and laborious duty in the obscure lot of minister of Crassy, in the mountains that separate the Pays de Vaud from the county of Burgundy. In the solitude of a sequestered village he bestowed a liberal, and even learned, education on his only daughter. She surpassed his hopes by her proficiency in the sciences and languages; and in her short visits to some relatives at Lausanne, the wit, the beauty, and erudition of Mademoiselle Curchod were the theme of universal applause. The report of such a prodigy awakened my curiosity. I saw and loved. I found her learned without pedantry, lively in conversation, pure in sentiment, and elegant in manners; and the first sudden emotion was fortified by the habits and knowledge of a more familiar acquaintance. She permitted me to make her two or three visits at her father's house. I passed some happy days there, in the mountains of Burgundy, and her parents honorably encouraged the connection. In a calm retirement the gay vanity of youth no longer fluttered in her bosom; she listened to the voice of truth and passion, and I might presume to hope that I had made some impression on a virtuous heart. At Crassy and Lausanne I indulged my dream of felicity; but on my return to England I soon discovered that my father would not hear of this strange alliance, and that without his consent I was myself destitute and helpless. After a painful struggle I yielded to my fate: I sighed as a lover, I obeyed as a son; my wound was insensibly healed by time, absence, and the habits of a new life. My cure was accelerated by a faithful report of the tranquillity and cheerfulness of the lady herself, and my love subsided in friendship and esteem. The minister of Crassy soon afterward died; his stipend died with him; his daughter retired to Geneva, where, by teaching young ladies, she earned a hard subsistence for herself and her mother; but in her lowest distress she maintained a spotless reputation and a dignified behavior. A rich banker of Paris, a citizen of Geneva, had the good fortune and good sense to discover and possess this inestimable treasure; and in the capital of taste and luxury she resisted the temptations of wealth, as she had sustained the hardships of indigence. The genius of her husband has exalted him to the most conspicuous station in Europe. In every change of prosperity and disgrace he has reclined on the bosom of a faithful friend; and Mademoiselle Curchod is now the wife of M. Necker, the minister, and perhaps the legislator, of the French monarchy."

To this narrative, Lord Sheffield, the editor of the "Memoirs," has added, in a note, the following extracts from Gibbon's journal:

"June, 1757.—I saw Mademoiselle Curchod. *Omnia vincit amor et nos cedamus amori.*

"August.—I went to Crassy, and staid two days.
"Sept. 15.—I went to Geneva.
"Oct. 15.—I came back to Lausanne, having passed through Crassy.
"Nov. 1.—I went to visit M. de Watteville at Loin, and saw Mademoiselle Curchod on my way through Rolle.
"Nov. 17.—I went to Crassy and staid there six days."

This is all that Gibbon himself has recorded of the affair, and his account is substantially correct. Still, owing to the lapse of time and the resulting errors of memory, it contains several inaccuracies and omits many important details. Mademoiselle Curchod was, as Gibbon relates, the only daughter of the Protestant minister of Crassier, or, as he writes it, Crassy, a village near Lausanne and a little way from the Lake of Geneva. She was born in 1737, and was, therefore, of nearly the same age as Gibbon. Contemporary accounts prove that he has not exaggerated her beauty and her accomplishments, nor the admiration that she excited wherever she appeared. While yet living at Crassy, she was courted by the ministers, young and old, who came to visit her father; and when she removed to Lausanne she became the acknowledged queen both of fashionable and of intellectual society there. She was made president of a literary organization called the *Académie des Eaux*, in which questions of sentiment as well as of letters were discussed; she shone at social gatherings, and, as often happens in little towns, she was followed in the streets by crowds of admirers, and by people, who said: "That is the pretty Mademoiselle Curchod." In a paper written for her *Académie* she gives the following description of herself:

"MY PORTRAIT.

"A face exhibiting youth and gayety; hair and complexion of a blonde, animated by blue, laughing, bright, and soft eyes; a small, but neat-shaped nose; a curling lip, whose smile accompanies that of the eyes with something of grace; a large and well-proportioned figure; but wanting in that enchanting elegance which augments its value, a rustic air in the deportment, and a certain brusqueness of movement, which contrasts prodigiously with a sweet voice and modest physiognomy. Such is the sketch of a picture which you may perhaps think to be too flattering."

That the picture was not more flattering than the truth appears from another description of Madame Necker, given by Sainte-Beuve in his "Galerie des Femmes Celèbres." Sainte-Beuve says of her that "she was beautiful, with that pure, virginal beauty which demands the freshness of youth. Her long and rather straight face was animated with a dazzling clearness and softened by her blue eyes, full of candor. Her slender waist had as yet only decent dignity, without stiffness and without training."

Naturally, this charming and accomplished Swiss girl made a profound impression upon an English youth like Gibbon, who was able to appreciate the beauty of her mind no less than the attractions of her person. It was equally natural that she should prefer him to her Swiss admirers. His external appearance, indeed, could scarcely have been prepossessing, for in his later years he is described as short in stature, fat to obesity, and with a face almost comical from its protuberant cheeks and little nose. His manners were ungraceful, and he confesses to small success in fencing and dancing. Here is a portrait of him from the pen of Mademoiselle Curchod, which, apparently, she forbore to complete:

"I will touch lightly on the countenance of M. G——. He has nice hair, a pretty hand, and the appearance of a man of good birth. His physiognomy is so intelligent and so remarkable that I do not know any one who resembles him. It has so much expression that one always discovers in it something new. His gestures, too, are so well-timed that they add a great deal to what he says. In a word, he has one of those extraordinary faces that one is never tired of examining, of picturing to one's self, and of mimicking. He knows the respect which is due to ladies. His politeness is easy, without being familiar. He dances passably. In a word, I recognize in him few of the charms which constitute the merit of a dandy. His talent varies prodigiously." . . .

But Gibbon, being a foreigner, had the advantage of a foreigner's distinction, and his intellectual ability compensated for his lack of the graces. Certain it is, that he was beloved, not, as he would lead his readers to infer, with a transient, superficial love, but with one that took a firm hold of Mademoiselle Curchod's heart. The proof of this exists in papers recently discovered in the archives of Coppet, the home of the Neckers after their exile from France, and they place Gibbon in the unenviable light of a man who did not know the value of the prize he had won, and who, by relinquishing it in tame submissiveness to his father, proved that he was incapable of true manly feeling.

Among the other documents preserved at Coppet are letters written by Gibbon to Mademoiselle Curchod, and some by her to him. The first from him has no special importance, and gives no indication of the relations of the pair; but it is followed by two which show clearly that something like an engagement existed at an early date between them. Of these letters, the first, written apparently after the week spent at Crassy, mentioned in the "Journal" under date of Nov. 17, 1757, contains this passage:

"I have always esteemed you highly, but the happy week which I spent at Crassier has given you a prominence in my mind which you had not before. I then saw all the treasures of the finest soul I know. The intellect and the passions are always on a level, and are proofs of a mind contented with itself. There is dignity even in its banter, and charms even in its seriousness. I saw you doing and saying the greatest things without being more aware of it than was necessary to enable you to do it intelligently. One sees plainly enough that your dominant passion is the liveliest tenderness towards the best of parents. It breaks out everywhere; and shows to all who come near you how susceptible your heart is of the noblest feelings. Every time this thought occurs to me it carries me far beyond the objects which first gave rise to it. I am at this moment reflecting upon the happiness of a man who, the possessor of a similar heart, finds you sensible to his tenderness, who can tell you a thousand times a day how much he loves you, and who never ceases to do it but in ceasing to live. I then build up schemes of happiness, fanciful perhaps, but which I would not exchange for anything that average mortals esteem greatest and most real."

In the letter following this we read :

"I have known you, mademoiselle, and everything has become changed to me. A felicity above that of empire, above even philosophy, may await me. But, alas, a punishment repeated every day, and each time aggravated by the thought of what I have lost, may fall to my lot. However, Socrates thanked the gods that he was born a Greek; and I, too, will thank them that I was born in an age, that I came to a country, in which I knew a woman whom my mind must always make me respect as the worthiest of her sex, while my heart makes me feel that she is also the most charming. 'O,' you will say, 'how serious he is! how melancholy and how tragical! What a tiresome man he is! Can I help yawning over his letter?' Yawn, mademoiselle, I feel that I have deserved it. But I deserve, also, that you should add, 'I wish all the preachers were as fully convinced of what they say as he who is now boring me and preaching to me.'"

These passages, it must be acknowledged, indicate anything but ardent passion. They are the compositions rather of a pedant than of a lover. Nor do some madrigals and sonnets, addressed by Gibbon to his mistress about this time, show anything more. They are artificial and cold, and unworthy of reproduction. That Gibbon already feared his father's disapproval of the match, and had prepared himself to give it up if necessary, appears from another letter, dated February 9, 1758, in which he says:

"How could you doubt for one moment of my love and my fidelity? Have you not read to the bottom of my soul a hundred times? Did you not see in it a passion as pure as it is strong? Have you not felt that your image would hold forever the first place in that heart which you now despise, and that, in the midst of pleasures, honors, and riches, I should enjoy nothing without you?

"While you were indulging in your suspicions, fortune was working for me—I do not dare to say for us. I found here a letter from my father, who has been expecting me a fortnight. He permits me to return to England, and I hasten thither as soon as I hear the zephyrs. It is true that, by a destiny peculiar to me, I see in the midst of a calm a storm rising. My father's letter is so kind, so affectionate; he shows such anxiety to see me again; he enlarges with so much pomp upon the projects that he has conceived for me, that it makes me imagine a thousand obstacles to my happiness, of a different nature and a different kind from those of the inequality of fortune, which alone formerly presented themselves to my mind.

"The condition, which the noblest principle made you exact, and which the tenderest motive led me to accept with pleasure, to take up my residence in this country—will with difficulty be listened to by my father, whose paternal love and whose ambition for his son will be equally shocked by it. Still, I do not yet despair of convincing him. Love will make me eloquent. He will desire my happiness; and if he does, he will not seek to separate me from you. My philosophy, or, rather, my temperament, makes me indifferent to riches. Honor is nothing to one who is not ambitious. If I know myself, I have never yet felt the attacks of this fatal passion. The love of study was my only passion until you made me feel that the heart has its needs as well as the mind, and that they consist in a reciprocal love. I learned to love, and you have not forbidden me to hope. What happier lot could I have than to see the time arrive when I can tell you, each instant, how much I love you, and to hear you say sometimes that I do not love an ingrate."

Mademoiselle Curchod's reply to this ominous communication was tender and womanly. She disclaims all desire to marry her lover against his father's wishes, but will wait for mitigating circumstances (*quelque espèce de palliatif*) to change the situation. To a hint in his letter that she was perhaps tired of the engagement, she replies that "this idea was too far removed from my heart to be present to my mind."

Two months after this, in April, 1758, Gibbon left Lausanne, and went to England for a protracted visit. His account of his intercourse with Mademoiselle Curchod conveys the impression that it ended with this departure, but it was not so. It is true that he never mentions her name in his journal, and that for four years there is no trace of any communication between him and her, except that he sent her a copy of his "Study of Literature," published in 1761.

By the death of her father, in 1760, she and her mother were left with no pecuniary resources beyond the trifling pension paid to the widow of a clergyman, and she was obliged to teach for a living; but though Gibbon knew this, there is no evidence that he ever rendered her assistance, or showed the slightest interest in her welfare. Still, that she must have written to him appears from a letter which he evidently intended should terminate their relations:

"MADEMOISELLE,—I cannot begin! and yet I must. I take up my pen. I put it down and take it up again. You perceive from this beginning what I am going to say. Spare me the rest. Yes, mademoiselle, I must renounce all thought of you forever. The decree is issued; my heart groans under it. But before my duty everything else must be silent."

He then repeats his father's objections to his marrying a foreigner and living abroad, and relates how he debated with himself for *two hours* before yielding. The letter continues:

"May you, mademoiselle, be more happy than I can ever hope to be. This will always be my prayer, it will even be my consolation. Would that I could contribute towards it by my wishes! I tremble to learn your fate; but, still, do not keep me in ignorance of it. It will be a cruel moment for me. Assure M. and Mme. Curchod of my respect, of my regard, and of my regrets. Adieu, mademoiselle. I shall always remember Mlle. Curchod as the noblest and most charming of women. May she never altogether forget a man who did not deserve the despair to which he is a victim!

"Adieu, mademoiselle. This letter may well appear strange to you, for it is the picture of my heart.

"I have written you twice on my way: at a village in Lorraine, once at Maestricht, likewise once from London. You have not received the letters. I do not know whether I may hope that this will reach you. I have the honor to be, with feelings that make the torment of my life, and an esteem that nothing can change, mademoiselle,

"Your very humble and very obedient servant,

"GIBBON.

"BURITON, August 24, 1762."

Explicit as this letter is in words, and equally decisive in its tone, it was not accepted as final by the loving woman to whom it was addressed. She hoped that something might yet happen to render her marriage with Gibbon possible, and she refused to believe that he had completely renounced her. When, therefore, a few months later, he came to Lausanne, she addressed to him a pathetic communication, the original of which is in the archives of Coppet, with the seal broken, as if it had been read by Gibbon and returned. At the bottom, in Mademoiselle Curchod's handwriting, are these words, in English: "A thinking soul is punishment enough, and every thought draws blood." The contents are these:

"MONSIEUR,—I blush at the step I am about to take. I would hide it from you. I would also hide it from myself. Is it possible, great God! that an innocent heart should so degrade itself? What a humiliation! I have had more terrible sorrows, but never one that I have felt more keenly. No matter, I am carried away in spite of myself. My own peace of mind demands this effort, and if I lose this present opportunity no peace will remain for me. Could I have it since the moment my heart, ever ingenious in tormenting itself, interpreted your marks of coldness as only proofs of your delicacy of feeling? For five whole years I have been sacrificing to this chimera by a unique and inconceivable conduct, but at last my mind, romantic as it is, has become convinced of its error. Upon my knees I beseech you to dissuade a maddened heart. Make a frank avowal of your complete indifference to me. My soul will adapt itself to the situation. Certainty will bring with it the tranquillity for which I sigh. If you refuse me this act of frankness, you will be the most contemptible of men, and God, who sees my heart, and who doubtless loves me, though he so sorely tries me—God, I say, will punish you in spite of my prayers, if there is the slightest evasion in your answer, or if, by your silence, you make a plaything of my peace.

"If you ever disclose this shameful step to any one in the world, were it my dearest friend, the horror of my punishment will condemn me for my fault. I shall look upon it as a fearful crime of which I did not know the atrociousness. Even now I feel it to be a baseness which outrages my modesty, my past conduct, and my present sentiments.

"GENEVA, 30th May."

What answer Gibbon made to this appeal beyond returning it nothing remains to show. But that Mademoiselle Curchod was in some way at last convinced of his faithlessness is proved by a subsequent letter from her, dated June 4, 1763, which commences

"MONSIEUR,—Five years of absence could not have produced the change that I have just experienced. I could have wished that you had written me sooner, or that your last letter but one had been couched in a different style. Exalted ideas, supported by an appearance of virtue, lead one to commit great errors. You ought to have spared me five or six irreparable ones, which will forever determine my lot in life. I know as well as you that this remark may seem to you neither tender nor delicate. For a long time past I have forgotten my pride, but I am delighted to regain enough of it to feel what I now reproach you with. Pardon me, however, and shed no tear over the hardships of my lot. My parents are dead; what is fortune to me? Besides, it was not to you that I sacrificed it, but to an imaginary creature who never existed save in a mind romantically distraught. For, as soon as your letter undeceived me, you became to me no more than any other man, and after having been the only one whom I could ever love, you became one of those for whom I had the least inclination, because you resemble the least my celadonic chimera. It remains only for you to make amends. Follow the plan of which you have given me the outlines. Join your attachment to that which my other friends show me. You will find me as confiding, as tender, and at the same time as indifferent, as I am for them."

She then communicates to him the distressed condition in which she was left by the death of both her father and her mother, and asks his advice about seeking employment in England as a lady's companion. That she still cherished a hope of winning him back appears both from what she says above about retaining him for a friend, and from a letter written with her approval, a few days before, by the pastor Moultou to the celebrated Rousseau, begging him to use his influence with Gibbon in her behalf. In this letter, a copy of which he seems to have sent to Mademoiselle Curchod, Moultou says to Rousseau: "How I pity this poor Mademoiselle Curchod. Gibbon, whom she loves, to whom she has sacrificed, I know, very good offers, has come to Lausanne, but cold, insensible, and as much cured of his old love as Mademoiselle C. is far from being. She has written me a letter which wrings my heart." He attributes Gibbon's coldness to some slanders of Mademoiselle Curchod, spread by a disappointed suitor, and asks Rousseau to contradict them, and to eulogize Mademoiselle Curchod to Gibbon. Rousseau took a common-sense view of the matter, and declined the commission. In his reply to Moultou, also dated June 4, 1763, he says, after unfavorably criticising Gibbon's writings, "Mr. Gibbon is no man for me. I cannot think him well adapted to Mademoiselle Curchod. He that does not know her value is unworthy of her; he that knows it and can desert her, is a man to be despised. She does not know what she is about. The man serves her more effectually than her own heart." Rousseau's letter was published during Gibbon's lifetime, and it appears to have annoyed him, for, in a note to his "Memoirs," he says: "As an author, I shall not appeal from the judgment or taste or caprice of *Jean Jacques;* but that extraordinary man, whom I admire and pity, should have been less precipitate in condemning the moral character and conduct of a stranger."

Nineteen days elapsed before Gibbon replied to Mademoiselle Curchod:

"LAUSANNE, 23d June, 1763.

"MADEMOISELLE, — Must you still continue to offer me happiness which reason compels me to renounce? I have lost your affection, though your friendship remains to me, and it does me too much honor for me to hesitate. I accept it, mademoiselle, as a precious exchange for mine, which is most perfectly yours, and as a treasure whose value I know too well ever to lose it. But this correspondence, mademoiselle, I feel its attractions, but, at the same time, I perceive all its dangers. I know it, as regards

THE FINAL RUPTURE.

myself, and I fear for both of us. Pray, let silence protect me. Excuse my fears, mademoiselle; they are founded on esteem."

He proceeds to discourage her from carrying out her project of going to England for employment, and ends with thanking her for a criticism of his "Study of Literature," saying that his delay in answering her had been occasioned by his desire to consider it.

Subsequently to this correspondence, the pair met at Voltaire's house at Ferney, and Gibbon seems to have angered Mademoiselle Curchod into a renewed expression of her opinion of his baseness. She wrote him a long letter, recounting the history of their engagement, and ended it by saying:

"I repeat, sir, that any heart which has once known mine and has ceased for one moment to love it was not worthy of it, and will never have my esteem. If I have otherwise expressed myself in speech or in writing, I now blush at it. It was the result of an indefinable sentiment, of a calmness, and of a disgusted indifference, and, above all, of the repugnance which one always feels at overthrowing one's idol.

"My conduct, you say, belies my words. In what? I ask. I am acting towards you as towards an honorable man of the world who is incapable of breaking his

word, of seducing, or of betraying; but who has been amusing himself with lacerating my heart by the best contrived and most skilfully managed tortures. I do not now threaten you with the anger of Heaven—an expression which escaped me, impulsively, but, without having the gift of prophecy, I can assure you that you will one day regret the irreparable loss you have suffered in alienating forever the too tender and the too open heart of S. C.
"Geneva, Sept. 21."

With this explosion of outraged affection and injured dignity Mademoiselle Curchod resigned herself to her fate, and in a little more than a year afterwards she married, as Gibbon tells us, Jacques Necker, then a partner in the great Paris banking firm of Thelusson & Necker, and subsequently minister of finance to Louis XVI. The marriage was brought about in a rather singular, though not unprecedented, manner. Mademoiselle Curchod, soon after her final rupture with Gibbon, despairing of all other means of livelihood, accepted the situation of companion to a rich young French widow, whom she met in Geneva, named De Vermenoux, and early in 1764 went to Paris with her. M. Necker, who was a native of Geneva, had been long a suitor for the hand of Madame de Vermenoux, and continued to pay her attention for some time after Mademoiselle Curchod became her companion. To relieve herself of his importunities, Madame de Vermenoux used her arts to make him marry Mademoiselle Curchod, saying, it is reported, "They will bore each other to death: that will give them something to do." At all events, she succeeded in making the match. Monsieur Necker fell in love with Mademoiselle Curchod, she accepted him, and the wedding was celebrated towards the end of the year.

As the wife of the wealthy and influential banker, Madame Necker at once took a prominent position in Paris society. Her house became famous. On Fridays she entertained artists and men of letters at dinner, which began at half-past four o'clock, and on Tuesdays she received her more fashionable friends. Among her regular Friday visitors were Marmontel, the journalist, poet, and playwright; Grimm, Diderot, and Morellet, the Encyclopædists; Suard, the Academician; the poet Dorat, the Abbé Galiani, St. Pierre, the author of "Paul et Virginie," which was read in manuscript in her *salon* before it was published; D'Alembert, the mathematician, and the naturalist Buffon. On Tuesdays she was visited by the poetess, Madame Geoffrin; the blind octogenarian beauty, Madame du Deffand; the Duchess de Lauzun; the Marquise de Créquy; the Maréchale de Luxembourg; Madame de Vermenoux, her old patroness; Madame de Marchais, Rousseau's beloved; the Countess d'Houdetot, and, in a word, by all the women in Paris worth knowing for their rank, beauty, wit, and accomplishments. Over this social and intellectual kingdom she reigned a queen, and like a queen, commanded respect as well as admiration. Her beauty, though not remarkable, was sufficient to produce a favorable first impression, and this impression she made permanent by the charm of her simple unaffected kindness of heart and of manner. Loving devotedly a husband who loved her as devotedly in return, the pair presented, in the midst of the corruption of Paris, a splendid example of conjugal fidelity, and, preserving the religious convictions of her childhood, she restrained by example and, when necessary, by rebuke, the audacious infidelity of both the men and the women by whom she was surrounded. A little tract by her in defence of Christianity, "Les Opinions Religieuses," had great success, and she wrote another against the lax views of marriage and divorce which characterized the times. Many other works proceeded from her pen, and a collection of them, embracing a copious journal kept by her, which was published after her death by her celebrated daughter, Madame de Staël, fills several volumes.

Among her admirers there were some whom Madame Necker inspired with an affection amounting almost to idolatry. The pastor Moultou, the friend of her youth, continued to be faithful to her. Thomas, a rough, self-educated peasant from Auvergne, was for twenty years her adoring slave, and the great Buffon, who made her acquaintance at the age of sixty-seven, five years after the death of a wife to whom he was tenderly attached, found in her society consolation for his widowed life, and often wrote to her expressing his admiration and affection. One of his letters commences thus:

"I have too deliciously enjoyed your letter, my adorable friend, to delay long imparting these delights of my heart. I could not get tired of reading and re-reading it. Lofty thoughts and profound sentiments are found in every line and are expressed in a manner so noble and so touching that not only am I impressed with them, but warmed, lifted to a point from whence I get a loftier idea of the nature of friendship. Ah, gods! it is not a sentiment without fire; on the contrary, it is a true warmth of soul, an emotion, a movement gentler but also livelier than that of any other passion; it is an untroubled enjoyment, a happiness rather than a pleasure; it is a communication of existence purer and yet more real than the sentiment of love; the union of souls is a mingling (*pénétration*); that of bodies is a simple contact."

This charming relation between Buffon and Madame Necker continued for thirteen years, and when her venerable friend fell dangerously ill, Madame Necker hastened to his bedside, and staid by it till his death. For five days she never left him, wiping from his face, with her own hands, the cold perspiration which his agony brought out on it, and rendering to him all the services of a daughter to a father.

Madame Necker's social reign in Paris lasted more than a quarter of a century. Monsieur Necker, who, when he married his wife, was simply a rich banker and a manager of the French East India Company, was made in 1777 director-general, or finance minister, by Louis XVI., and held the post until 1781, when he resigned because a seat in the royal council was denied him on account of his being a Protestant. Recalled in 1788, he held office until 1789, when his dismissal by the king having provoked a popular uprising, he was again reinstated; but, losing all hope of saving the monarchy, and becoming unpopular because of his efforts in its behalf, he finally withdrew from Paris in 1790, and took up his residence at his château of Coppet, in Switzerland, where he spent the remainder of his life.

Not the least gratifying advantage which Madame Necker derived from her elevated position was the means it afforded her of proving to Gibbon how great a mistake he had made in not securing her for himself.

Her prophetic last words to him, "You will one day regret the irreparable loss you have suffered in alienating forever the too tender and the too open heart of S. C.," were now fulfilled. In the autumn of 1765, Gibbon came over to visit her at Paris, and she had the gratification of being able to write to a friend:

"I do not know whether I told you that I have seen Gibbon. I cannot express the pleasure it gave me, not that I have any remains of sentiment for a man whom I believe to be unworthy of it, but my feminine vanity never had a more complete and honorable triumph. He staid two weeks in Paris. I had him every day at my house. He had become gentle, submissive, and decent even to prudery. Continual witness of my husband's tenderness, of his talent and his devotion, a zealous admirer of wealth, he caused me to notice for the first time that which surrounds me, and which, if it had impressed me at all, had impressed me only disagreeably."

That this burst of exultation was justified appears from Gibbon's own account. Of this same visit he writes to his friend Holroyd, afterwards Lord Sheffield

"The Curchod (Madame Necker) I saw at Paris.

She was very fond of me, and the husband particularly civil. Could they insult me more cruelly? Ask me every evening to supper, go to bed, and leave me alone with his wife—what an impertinent security! It is making an old lover of mighty little consequence. She is as handsome as ever and much genteeler; seems pleased with her fortune rather than proud of it."

We have, probably, in these two bits of concurrent testimony, the key to Gibbon's otherwise inexplicable behavior towards Mademoiselle Curchod. He was luxurious, self-indulgent, and a worshipper of wealth, not as mere wealth, but for the comforts which it commands. His complaints of Swiss living and cooking, his eulogy of English housekeeping, the keenness he shows in making bargains and his frequent references, in his correspondence with Lord Sheffield, to his investments, all prove this, while his timidity of character appears from his own confession that he never had the courage to speak in Parliament. That such a man, not certain of his own worldly future, should shrink from marriage with a poor Swiss girl was only natural; and when he found her rich, influential, and admired in the foremost city of Europe, it was equally natural that his esteem for her, if not his affection, should revive.

Gibbon, on his part, was destined to a career no less brilliant than Madame Necker's. His first published work, the "Study of Literature," had little success, and he abandoned, as we have seen, his projected history of the Swiss republics after writing the first few chapters. But in his twenty-eighth year, sitting, as he tells us, "amidst the ruins of the Capitol at Rome, while the barefooted friars were singing vespers in the temple of Jupiter transformed into a Christian church," the idea of describing the decline and fall of the city entered his mind, though it was not until 1768, four years later, when he had finally renounced his Swiss history, that he seriously undertook the task. Preliminary study and research, interrupted by the death of his father and the labor required to settle his deeply embarrassed estate, consumed four years more, and only in 1772, when he had reached the age of thirty-four, was he able to begin the work of composition. It took another four years to complete the first volume. "Many experiments were made," he says, "before I could hit the middle tone between a dull chronicle and a rhetorical declamation. Three times did I compose the first chapter and twice the second and third, before I was tolerably satisfied with their effect." His practice was "to cast a long paragraph in a single mould, to try it by my ear, to deposit it in my memory, but to suspend the action of the pen till I had given the last polish to the work." When he had thus laboriously perfected his composition he was satisfied with it, and sent it directly to the printer without submitting to the criticism of others, because, as he says, "The author is the best judge of his own performance. No one has so deeply meditated on the subject; no one is so sincerely interested in the event."

The success which the book had, is paralleled only by that of Macaulay's "History of England," a century afterwards. The first edition was exhausted in a few days, a second and a third were as quickly disposed of, and its author was overwhelmed with praise, not only from his personal friends, but from other historians, like Hume and Robertson. His treatment of the Christian religion provoked a swarm of attacks, only one of which he found it necessary to answer, and that merely because the writer had impugned his literary honesty. The fame he acquired led to political promotion. He was already a member of Parliament, but now he was employed by the ministry to defend their measures with his pen, and as a reward for his efforts was made by Lord North one of the Lords of Trade, an office which he retained until the fall of his patron in 1783, when he retired altogether from political life.

It thus became Gibbon's turn to show Madame Necker that she, too, had lost something in losing him for a husband. The first volume of his "History" had appeared in March, 1776, and in May the Neckers came over to London on a visit. Gibbon devoted himself to entertaining them, but his attitude towards them was no longer so humble as it had been in 1765. He wrote to his friend Holroyd:

CORRESPONDENCE RENEWED.

"At present I am very busy with the Neckers. I live with her just as I used to do twenty years ago, laugh at her Paris varnish and oblige her to become a simple, reasonable Suissesse. The man, who might read English husbands lessons of proper and dutiful behaviour, is a sensible, good-natured creature."

On her part, Madame Necker seems to have experienced a revival of affection for her quondam lover, and upon her return to Paris she wrote to him:

"You ought not to doubt of the pleasure which I take in your success, for I have long been warned of my *amour propre* only by my sensibility. I will not give you advice. I could only criticise your opinions or your sentiments, and no advice could change them. Besides, you have a style of writing peculiar to yourself. You must follow the promptings of your genius, and whoever would risk advising you to do anything but giving up to yourself, would be unworthy of admiring you, and of feeling the inestimable value of a sublime singularity."

A month later she writes again, praising his history, and begging him to come and take up his residence in Paris as the only place worthy to be honored by his presence. She adds

"You, who have transferred to English all the delicacy, the finesse, and at the same time the lucidity of our tongue, will transfer to French the richness and strength of yours, and you will write both with that harmonious pen which seems to place words only to charm the ear, as a skilful hand touches the keys of a harpsichord.

"But when will you come? Monsieur, fix for us the precise day that we may enjoy it in advance. Monsieur Necker and I both present to you the assurance of the distinguished sentiments which we have vowed to you for life."

Madame du Deffand also wrote to him about this time a letter in which she says: "I have seen very little of M. and Mme. Necker since your departure. I supped once as a third with them, and Madame Necker has supped once with me. We talk of M. Gibbon, and of what else? Of M. Gibbon, always of M. Gibbon."

The invitation so flatteringly given was accepted the following year, and Gibbon was highly delighted with the treatment he received. He writes to Lord Sheffield:

"You remember that the Neckers were my principal dependence, and the reception which I have met with from them very far surpassed my most sanguine expectations. I do not indeed lodge in this house (as it might incite the jealousy of the husband and procure me a *lettre de cachet*), but I live very much with them, and dine and sup whenever they have company, which is almost every day, and whenever I like it, for they are not in the least *exigeans*."

After his return to England Gibbon must have been absorbed in his work and the Neckers occupied with the political troubles of France, for no correspondence seems to have passed between them until 1781, when he sent to Madame Necker the second and the third volume of his history with a letter, in which, referring to their early love affair, he says:

"I am sufficiently punished by the reflection that my conduct may have laid me open to a reproach which my heart alone can contradict. No, madame, I shall never forget the dearest moments of my youth, and its pure and indelible memory is now lost in the truest and most unalterable friendship. After a long separation I had the happiness of being able to spend six months in your company. Every day added to the feelings of respect and of gratitude with which you inspired me, and I quitted Paris with the firm but vain resolution always to keep up a correspondence which alone could compensate me for what I had lost."

Madame Necker's reply is most affectionate. Gently chiding Gibbon for having so long neglected to write to her, she says:

"Although I am concentrated in the objects of my tenderest attachment, the sensibility which I have received from nature suffices for other ties. My soul exists only when it loves, and when it still lacks new means of existence outside of its centre. I want you to bestow on me the sentiments you promised. I reckoned on them in making up my sum of happiness. I know you; you will have affection for me when you see me again, and you will not be conscious of your faults until you have them no longer."

Two years later, on his retirement from politics, Gibbon removed permanently from England to Switzerland, and took up his residence in Lausanne, in a house which he occupied jointly with his friend Deyverdun. Here, in full view of the beautiful Lake of Geneva and of the Savoy Alps, he remained several years, engaged upon his "Decline and Fall," the last volume of which he completed in 1787, and in enjoying the society of his friends. That in this paradise his loneliness, like that of Adam, began to weary him, appears from what he says in 1784 in a letter to Lord Sheffield:

"Should you be very much surprised to hear of my being married? Amazing at it may seem, I do assure you that the event is less improbable than it would have appeared to myself a twelvemonth ago. Deyverdun and I have often agreed, in jest and in earnest, that a house like ours would be regulated, graced, and enlivened by an agreeable female companion; but each of us seems desirous that his friend should sacrifice himself for the public good."

Again, in 1790, he writes to the same friend:

"Sometimes, in a solitary mood, I have fancied myself married to one or another of those whose society and conversation are the most pleasing to me; but when I have painted in my fancy all the probable consequences of such a union, I have started from my dream, rejoiced in my escape, and ejaculated a thanksgiving that I was still in the possession of my natural freedom. Yet I feel, and I shall continue to feel, that domestic solitude, however it may be alleviated by work, by study, and even by friendship, is a comfortless state, which will grow more painful as I descend in the vale of years."

And again in 1791:

"I wish it were in my power to give you an adequate idea of the conveniency of my house and the beauty of my garden, both of which I have improved at a considerable expense since the death of poor Deyverdun. But the loss of a friend is indeed irreparable. Were I ten years younger, I might possibly think of a female companion ; but the choice is difficult, the success doubtful, the engagement perpetual, and at fifty-four a man should never think of altering the whole system of his life and habits."

The storm that burst upon the French monarchy drove, as we have seen, the Neckers into exile, and Coppet, where they went to live, was not far from Lausanne. Madame Necker, preserving her tenderness for the object of her early attachment, sought by every feminine art to lure him to her side, and in a measure succeeded. Here is what she writes to him in 1792, referring to a visit he had made her :

"We think often of the days, full of charms, which we passed with you at Geneva. I felt during all this time a sentiment that was new to me, perhaps it would be also new to many people. By a rare favour of Providence I reunited in one and the same spot one of the sweet and pure affections of my youth and also that which now constitutes my lot upon earth, and which makes it so enviable. This peculiarity, joined with the pleasures of an incomparable conversation, formed for us a sort of enchantment, and the connection of the past with the present made all my days appear like a dream, proceeding from the ivory gate for the consolation of mortals. Will you not help us to prolong it?"

At the same time she could not resist the temptation to unsheathe the claw beneath the velvet, and to give him a peculiarly feminine scratch. We have seen how, in the loneliness of his bachelor home, Gibbon's thoughts turned towards matrimony, and there is an unverified legend that he actually once offered himself at Lausanne to an English woman, Lady Elizabeth Foster, afterwards Duchess of Devonshire, who, like many of her countrywomen, had called to pay her respects to the celebrated historian. The legend narrates that he got upon his knees to make his offer, and when, upon being rejected, he attempted to rise, he was so fat and infirm that he was unable to do it, and had to be helped up by his servants. Referring to this matrimonial inclination, Madame Necker goes on to say:

"Monsieur de Germain has thought fit to marry,

and he has had to renounce much of his attentions. Beware, monsieur, of these late bonds. The marriage which makes one happy in ripe age is that which was contracted in youth. Then only is the union perfect, tastes are shared, sentiments expand, ideas become common, the intellectual faculties mutually shape themselves. All life is double, and all life is a prolongation of youth, for the impressions of the soul govern the eyes, and the beauty which has passed away preserves its empire, but for you, monsieur, in all the vigour of thinking, when your whole existence is fixed, a worthy wife could not be found without a miracle, and an imperfect association recalls always Horace's statue in which a beautiful head is joined to the body of a stupid fish."

Her other letters to him written about this time also manifest a lively interest in his welfare. Here are some extracts:

"You have always been dear to me, but the friendship you show to M. Necker increases that which you inspire in me for so many other reasons, and I love you at present with a double affection."

"Your words are for me the milk and honey of the promised land, and I seem to hear their sweet murmur. Still, I yet regret the pleasure that I had of entertaining you during the day with my thoughts of the day before. I lived thus with you, doubly, in the past and in the present, and the one embellished the other. May I flatter myself that I shall find again this happiness in our avenues of Coppet?"

"What price does not my heart attach to your health, and the interest which your friendship sheds upon our retreat! On arriving here, on finding only the tombs of those whom I so much loved, you were to me a solitary tree, whose shade still covers the desert which separates me from the past years of my life.

"You promised me to read 'Les Opinions Religieuses,' and whatever may be your metaphysical opinions, I am sure you will be struck by the chapter on happiness. The touching word which ends your letter convinces me of it. I want to add to it these lines of *Zaïre*:

'Généreux, bienfaisant, juste, plein de vertus.
S'il était né Chrétien, que serait-il de plus.'

"Return to us when you are left to yourself. It is the moment which ought always to belong to *your first and to your last friend*. I cannot discover which of these titles is the sweetest, and the dearest to my heart."

This affectionate intercourse appears to have been kept up both in person and by correspondence until the end. Madame Necker's last letter to Gibbon is dated Dec. 9, 1793, and he died Jan. 16, 1794. She, too, died the following May, after months of suffering which incapacitated her for writing. It would have been romantic, if it could be said that her last thoughts were of Gibbon, but, in truth, they were exclusively of her husband, whom she loved to the day of her death as truly and as tenderly as she had loved him from the beginning of their married life. Her body was interred at Coppet, where it has ever since remained. Gibbon's was entombed in Lord Sheffield's family vault in England. The pair were thus divided in death as they were in early life, the native country of each claiming and receiving its own.

DR. SAMUEL JOHNSON.

DR. JOHNSON AND MRS. THRALE.

Dr. Johnson's acquaintance with Mrs. Thrale began in January, 1765, when he was fifty-six years of age and she was twenty-four. Mr. Thrale was a wealthy brewer, who had received a liberal education, and, as well as his wife, had a fondness for the society of literary men and of artists. The couple, who had been married only a few months, took such a liking to Johnson that they made him their intimate friend, and for the remaining sixteen years of Mr. Thrale's life he lived for the greater part of the time at their villa at Streatham, near London. A chamber was set apart for him, which he occupied for several days of every week, his tastes in eating and drinking were sedulously consulted, conveniences were provided for his experiments in chemistry, the library was put under his care, with a liberal allowance of money for the purchase of books, he was consulted in the management of Mr. Thrale's business affairs, and, in short, he became an integral member of the family. His fame and the hospitality of the Thrales made the house the favorite resort of the finest minds in London, and as Abraham Hayward says in his memoirs of Mrs. Thrale: "Holland House, alone and in its best days, would convey to persons living in our time an adequate conception of the Streatham circle when it comprised Burke, Reynolds, Garrick, Goldsmith, Boswell, Murphy, Dr. Burney and his daughter, Mrs. Montague, Mrs. Boscawen, Mrs. Crewe, Lord Loughborough, Dunning (afterwards Lord Ashburton), Lord Mulgrave, Lord Westcote, Sir Lucas, and Mr. (afterwards Sir William) Pepys, Major Holroyd (afterwards Lord Sheffield), the Bishop of London and Mrs. Porteous, the Bishop of Peterborough and Mrs. Hinchcliff, Miss Gregory, Miss Streatfield, etc." In this literary elysium Johnson's life, as may well be imagined, passed most agreeably. His health and his spirits improved, and he enjoyed himself to the full. Mr. Thrale's death in 1781 put an end to it all. The Streatham establishment was broken up, and though Dr. Johnson occasionally visited Mrs. Thrale at her town residence, and continued to correspond with her, the intimacy gradually lessened, until, upon her marriage to Gabriel Piozzi in 1784, six months before Johnson's death, it ceased altogether.

Mrs. Thrale, like Dr. Johnson, is best known to the world through the medium of Boswell's life of the distinguished scholar. That incomparable work, unique among biographies, has probably a hundred readers where any other on the same subject has one, and naturally it has had a predominant influence in shaping public opinion. Boswell, who was an admiring worshipper of Johnson and a jealous rival of Mrs. Thrale, hated her because Johnson liked her, and because he foresaw that she, too, would write a memoir of his hero in competition with his own. Hence he persistently represents her in the most unfavorable light, and impugns both the soundness of her understanding and the accuracy of her recollections. Above all, he has succeeded in establishing the belief that, after the death of her husband, she treated Dr. Johnson with ingratitude, and that her marriage with Piozzi was a sacrifice of self-respect to an unworthy passion. The truth is that Dr. Johnson was indebted to Mrs. Thrale, not only for the kindness which, as he himself acknowledged in the very paroxysm of his anger at her re-marriage, " soothed twenty years of a life radically wretched," but for an intellectual companionship and stimulus which materially assisted in making his reputation. Even Boswell has the candor to say: " The vivacity of Mrs. Thrale's literary talk aroused him to cheerfulness and exertion, even when they were alone. But this was not often the case; for he found here a constant succession of what gave him the highest enjoyment; the society of the learned, the witty, and the eminent in every way, who were assembled in numerous companies, called forth his wonderful powers, and gratified him with admiration, to which no man could be insensible."

Johnson, therefore, owed Mrs. Thrale quite as much as she owed him, and that, after her husband's death, her intimacy with him came to an end, was no proof of ingratitude. Nor was her marriage with Piozzi at all deserving of censure. Piozzi, though only an Italian music master, was in every way as worthy a man as Thrale, and made a much better husband. In the light that modern inquiry has thrown upon the subject, the conviction cannot be avoided that Mrs. Thrale's real offence was preferring the younger and handsomer Italian to her elderly admirer, and that Johnson's resentment was merely the commonplace effect of a lover's rejection. He was, probably, not himself aware of the nature of his feelings, nor does it appear that any of his friends suspected it. If they did, they did not choose to say so. Nor did Mrs. Thrale ever suggest this explanation of Johnson's conduct, and in the two volumes of correspondence with him which she published after his death, nothing is found to support it. By common consent it seems to have been agreed to represent the quarrel as having had reference solely to Piozzi's position and character, and to leave everything else out of consideration. This is done by even so well-informed a writer as Lord Macaulay, and the only eminent author who has expressed a different opinion is Lord Brougham, who, in his "Lives of Men of Letters," ventures the surmise that "Johnson was, perhaps unknown to himself, in love with Mrs. Thrale."

All accounts agree in depicting Mrs. Thrale as a woman in every way deserving of admiration. Though not positively beautiful, she was pretty enough at the age of fourteen to be selected by Hogarth to sit for the principal figure in his picture "The Lady's Last Stake," while the vivacity of her countenance and the graciousness of her manners rendered her otherwise attractive. Her intellectual gifts were uncommon. When she was thirteen her parents, who were in comfortable circumstances, though not wealthy, placed her under the tuition of the learned Dr. Arthur Collier,

MRS. THRALE.

and by him she was taught Latin, Spanish, and Italian, besides other branches of knowledge. Moreover, notwithstanding his sixty odd years, he inspired in her, as he did in another of his girl pupils, Sophy Streatfield, a romantic affection. She says of him: "A friendship more tender, or more unpolluted by interest or by vanity, never existed; love had no place at all in the connection, nor had he any rival but my mother." Whether from jealousy or from prudence, her mother, however, thought it best to part her from her adored preceptor, lest his influence over her should prevent her marriage. As for Miss Streatfield, she took him, when he became so old as to be infirm, into her own home, he died in her arms, and for years she marked the anniversary of his death by wearing black.

How Mrs. Thrale profited by Dr. Collier's instruction is proved by her subsequent career. Besides her familiarity with English literature and a knowledge of French, Italian, and Spanish, the Rev. E. Mangin, who knew her during the last eight or ten years of her life, says that "she not only read and wrote Hebrew, Greek, and Latin, but had for sixty years constantly and ardently studied the Scriptures and the works of commentators in the original languages." This is an exaggeration, but that her learning was considerable and her information varied and extensive, Boswell's reports of her disputes with Dr. Johnson abundantly show. On several occasions she proved her knowledge of Latin by translating it into English offhand, and Dr. Johnson did not disdain her co-operation in making a series of English versions of the Latin odes of Boethius, which are printed with her second volume of his letters. After one of their frequent intellectual contests, he said to her, in reply to an apologetic remark, " Madam, you never talk nonsense. You have as much sense and more wit than any woman I know." Miss Reynolds has also left the following testimony to his appreciation of her:

"On the praises of Mrs. Thrale he used to dwell with a peculiar delight, a paternal fondness, expressive of conscious exultation in being so intimately acquainted with her. One day, in speaking of her to Mr. Harris, author of 'Hermes,' and expatiating on

MRS. THRALE'S ATTRACTIONS.

her various perfections—the solidity of her virtues, the brilliancy of her wit, and the strength of her understanding, etc.—he quoted some lines, with which he concluded his most eloquent eulogium, of which I retained but the two last:

" Virtues of such a generous kind,
Good in the last recesses of the mind."

Madame d'Arblay (Fanny Burney), the famous author of " Evelina," also wrote of her after her death:

"She was, in truth, a most wonderful character for talents and eccentricity, for wit, genius, generosity, spirit, and powers of entertainment. She had a great deal both of good and not good, in common with Mme. de Staël Holstein. They had the same sort of highly superior intellect, the same depth of learning, the same general acquaintance with science, the same ardent love of literature, the same thirst for universal knowledge, and the same buoyant animal spirits, such as neither sickness, sorrow, nor even terror could subdue. Their conversation was equally luminous from the sources of their own fertile minds and from their splendid acquisitions from the acquirements of others."

From other sources we learn that in conversation she was accounted a formidable rival to the celebrated blue-stocking, Mrs.

Montague, and the verses, letters, and other productions she left behind her evince more than ordinary literary skill.

Johnson, on his part, was remarkable for his repulsive person and uncouth manners. Boswell says: "Miss Porter told me that when he was first introduced to her mother his appearance was very forbidding. He was then lean and lank, so that his immense structure of bones was hideously striking to the eye, and the scars of scrofula were deeply visible. He also wore his hair, which was straight and stiff, separated behind, and he often had seemingly convulsive starts and odd gesticulations, which tended to excite at once surprise and ridicule." Madame d'Arblay, who first saw him when he was sixty, also speaks of his "perpetual convulsive movements, either of his hands, lips, feet, and knees, and sometimes of all together." His behavior at table was what we should call disgusting. He ate ravenously, like a half-famished man, and, while making pretence to nicety, he preferred quantity to quality. Lord Chesterfield, in one of his letters to his son, describes him, without mentioning his name, as "a respectable Hottentot," and, after speaking of the defects of his person already mentioned, goes on to say: "He throws anywhere but down his throat whatever he means to drink, and only mangles what he means to carve. Inattentive to all the regards of social life, he mistimes or misplaces everything. He disputes with heat and indiscriminately, mindless of the rank, character, and situation of those with whom he disputes, absolutely ignorant of the several gradations of familiarity or respect." An Irish clergyman, Dr. Campbell, who dined with Johnson at Mrs. Thrale's in 1775, writes of him: "He has the aspect of an idiot, without the faintest ray of sense gleaming from any one feature—with the most awkward gait, an unpowdered gray wig on one side of his head—he is forever dancing the devil's jig, and sometimes he makes the most drivelling effort to whistle some thought in his absent paroxysms."

All this is confirmed by Boswell, who recounts numerous instances of Johnson's slovenliness, rudeness, and general ill manners. Yet his colossal stature, great physical strength, and manly courage impressed his female friends with that sense of power which is so attractive to their sex. On the one occasion when he followed the hounds, his fearless riding elicited general admiration, and when two large dogs were fighting in his presence, he separated them by taking one in each hand and holding them apart at arm's-length. At another time, merely to display his agility, he climbed over a high gate which came in his way; and Foote, the actor, having announced that he would caricature him on the stage, he prevented it by the significant purchase of a stout oaken stick.

In spite, therefore, of his repulsive appearance and behavior, Johnson had compensating physical advantages, and these were amply re-enforced by his intellectual gifts. Like ugly John Wilkes, he was "only half an hour behind the handsomest man in England." Mrs. Porter, whom he married, remarked after her first interview with him: "Mr. J. is the most sensible man that I ever saw in my life." Mrs. Kitty Clive, the famous actress, said: "I love to sit by Dr. Johnson; he always entertains me." The aged Countess of Eglintoune was so pleased with him that she gave this message to Boswell: "Tell Johnson I love him exceedingly." Miss Adams, a daughter of Dr. Adams of Pembroke College, Oxford, writes to a friend in the last year of Johnson's life: "Dr. Johnson, though not in good health, is in general very talkative, and infinitely agreeable and entertaining." Mrs. Cotton testifies that: "Dr. Johnson, despite his rudeness, was at all times delightful, having a manner peculiar to himself in relating anecdotes that could not fail to attract both old and young." Mr. Langton told Boswell of an evening gathering, where ladies of the highest rank and fashion gathered round Johnson's chair, four and five deep, to hear him talk. Madame d'Arblay had for him a feeling bordering upon idolatry. Her diary abounds in expressions like these: "My dear, dear Dr. Johnson! what a charming man you are!" "But Dr. Johnson's approbation! it almost crazed me with agreeable surprise." "I have so true a veneration for him that the very sight of him inspires me with delight and reverence." "But how grateful do I feel to this dear Dr. Johnson." "Dear, dear, and much reverenced Dr. Johnson!" "This day was the ever-honored, ever-lamented Dr. Johnson committed to the earth. Oh, how sad a day to me! I could not keep my eyes dry all day! Nor can I now in the recollecting." And four years afterwards she says of a conversation about him with Mr. Wyndham: "My praise of him was of a more solid kind—his principles, his piety, his kind heart under all its rough coating; but I need not repeat what I said. My dear friends know every word."

Women liked also in Johnson his delicate gallantry. He had a tender, respectful love for them, and succeeded in making them feel it. Mrs. Thrale once said to him: "Your compliments, sir, are made seldom, but when they are made, they have an elegance unequalled." To her, assuredly, he paid homage in the most flattering manner, wrote sonnets in her honor, both in English and in Latin; when he was absent he kept up a constant correspondence with her, and he contrived even in the violence of his contradiction to make that contradiction a tribute to her understanding. Goldsmith, who knew him well, and who, as often as anybody, suffered from his rudeness, said of him: "He has nothing of the bear but his skin."

It was not without reason, therefore, that Boswell writes:

"Let not my readers smile to think of Johnson's being a candidate for female favor. Mr. Peter Garrick assured me that he was told by a lady that in her opinion Johnson was 'a very seducing man.' Disadvantages of person and manner may be forgotten where intellectual pleasure is communicated to a susceptible mind, and Johnson was capable of feeling the most delicate and disinterested attachment."

That Dr. Johnson was indeed capable of ardent love for women there is no doubt. Boswell strives to portray him as a man of mighty intellect, raised by it above ordinary human weaknesses. But even Boswell, with the unconscious fidelity of a photographer, has incidentally preserved many traits of Johnson's character which redeem it from being that of a faultless monster, and exhibit it in a more human aspect. He admits that "Johnson had from his youth been sensible to the influence of female charms;" and specifying several of the objects of his boyish love, he introduces the account of his early marriage with this remark: "In a man whom religious education has secured from licentious indulgences, the passion of love, when it once has seized him, is exceedingly strong, being unimpaired by dissipation and totally concentrated in one object. This was experienced by Johnson when he became the fervent admirer of Mrs. Porter after her first husband's death."

Johnson's impressibility by feminine charms and his own consciousness of it are evinced by a remark he made at the age of forty to his friend and former pupil, David Garrick: "I'll come no more behind your scenes, David; for the silk stockings and white bosoms of your actresses excite my amorous propensities." After the famous dinner at Mr. Dilly's, to which Johnson was inveigled to meet Mr. Wilkes, Boswell records that a pretty Quakeress, Mrs.

Knowles, being present, "Mr. Wilkes held a candle to show a fine print of a beautiful female figure which hung in the room, and pointed out the elegant contour of the bosom with the finger of an arch connoisseur. He afterwards, in a conversation with me, waggishly insisted that all the time Johnson showed visible signs of a fervent admiration of the corresponding charms of the fair Quaker." At seventy-two he remarked to Boswell: "Sir, it is a very foolish resolution to resolve not to marry a pretty woman. Beauty is of itself very estimable. No, sir, I would prefer a pretty woman unless there are objections to her."

Elsewhere Boswell says:

"When I told him that a young and handsome countess had said to me: 'I should think that to be praised by Dr. Johnson would make one a fool all one's life,' and that I answered, 'Madam, I shall make him a fool to-day by repeating this to him.' He said, 'I am too old to be made a fool, but if you say I am made a fool I shall not deny it. I am much pleased with a compliment, especially from a pretty woman.'"

And again, speaking of a visit to a Hebrides chief, Boswell records:

"This evening, one of our married ladies, a lively, pretty little woman, good humoredly sat down upon Dr. Johnson's knee, and, being encouraged by some of the company, put her hands round his neck and kissed him. 'Do it again,' said he, 'and let us see who will tire first.' He kept her on his knee some time, while he and she drank tea."

Another acquaintance of Johnson's relates that "Two young women from Staffordshire visited him when I was present to consult him on the subject of Methodism, to which they were inclined. 'Come,' said he, 'you pretty fools, dine with me and Maxwell at the Mitre, and we will talk over that subject,' which they did, and after dinner he took one of them upon his knee and fondled her for half an hour together."

It would be a mistake, nevertheless, to infer from these anecdotes that Johnson, as regards women, was coarse and sensual. He appreciated more the finer elements of the feminine character, and took delight in the society of cultivated ladies. Mrs. Thrale herself relates that "when Mr. Thrale once asked Johnson which had been the happiest period of his life, he replied: 'It was that

DELICACY OF FEELING. 63

year in which he spent one whole evening with Molly Aston. 'That, indeed,' he said, 'was not happiness, it was rapture, but the thought of it sweetened the whole year.' I must add that the evening alluded to was not passed *tête-à-tête*, but in a select company of which the present Lord Kilmorey was one." Of another lady, Miss Boothby, Mrs. Thrale writes : " Johnson told me she pushed her piety to bigotry, her devotion to enthusiasm ; that she somewhat disqualified herself for the duties of this life by her perpetual aspirations after the next. Such, however, was the purity of her mind, he said, and such the graces of her manner, that he and Lord Lyttelton used to strive for her preference with an emulation that occasioned hourly disgust and ended in lasting animosity." His romantic love for his wife while she lived and his devotion to her memory long after her death, are frequently mentioned in Boswell's pages. His affection for Mrs. Thrale was evidently inspired by her mind rather than by her person, and all the letters he wrote to her are most chivalrous. Of ladies' dress he was, notwithstanding his nearsightedness, an appreciative critic. Boswell relates that on one occasion he was greatly displeased because Mrs. Thrale appeared before him in a dark-colored gown. "You little creatures," he said, "should not wear those sort of colors; they are unsuitable in every way. What! have not all insects gay colors?" When none of the ladies could explain why a pale lilac should be called a *soupir etouffé*, he was ready with the answer: "It is called a stifled sigh because it is checked in its progress, and is only half a color." Elsewhere Mrs. Thrale informs us:

"It was indeed astonishing how he could remark with a sight so miserably imperfect; but no accidental position of a riband escaped him, so nice was his observation and so rigorous his demands of propriety. When I went with him to Lichfield, and came down stairs to breakfast at the inn, my dress did not please him, and he made me alter it entirely before he would stir a step with me about the town."

In like manner Madame d'Arblay says he once refused to go to church at Streatham with her mother until she had changed a hat which he disliked for one that suited him better.

There was enough, therefore, in the characters of both Mrs. Thrale and Dr. Johnson, notwithstanding their disparity of age, to make them pleased with each other. The same intellectual strength and cultivation which rendered Dr. Collier so dear to her in her girlhood she found in a larger degree in the person of her new friend, while he in turn was flattered by her admiration and grateful for her affection. Besides this, she had a special reason for drawing close to him. Her husband, though he was possessed of superior abilities, and had been educated at Oxford in the society of young men of good family, yet lacked the refinement necessary to preserve her love. A wife was to him a companion and a housekeeper and the mother of his children, and that was all. He treated her as a despot treats a slave. "I know no man," said Johnson to Boswell, "who is more master of his wife and family than Thrale. If he holds up a finger he is obeyed." He introduced into his house as a constant guest an illegitimate son, and appointed him one of his executors. He made love to a pretty girl, the Sophy Streatfield already mentioned, before his wife's face; and at a time when, if ever, she deserved consideration, he made her exchange seats at table with her rival, who occupied one exposed to a draught.

Nor was he intellectually so superior to her as to justify this domination. Even in business matters he committed many blunders, which, with Dr. Johnson's counsel, she aided him to repair, and she did her best to repress in him the gluttony, the indulgence of which eventually caused his death. Johnson, on the other hand, as all the evidence shows, was tender and sympathetic. He took an interest in her little ambitions, shared her sorrows, and consoled her in her afflictions, of which the frequent loss of children was not the least.

Given thus, on the one hand, a man of vigorous intellect, strong, though controlled passions, and fascinating conversation, and, on the other, a woman of talent, able and quick to appreciate his merits, and let the two be thrown together intimately for the period of sixteen years, nothing would be more natural than for a feeling to spring up, at least on the part of the man, warmer than mere friendship. Difference of age counts for little in such cases, for it is a common saying that the heart never grows old. A man in Johnson's position readily forgets how he actually appears to the woman who flatters and pleases him, and, conscious only of his own youthful feelings, is prone to imagine that he seems to her as young as he does to himself. There is no proof that Mrs. Thrale ever entertained any sentiment for Johnson other than the esteem which in Madame d'Arblay became reverent adoration. Indeed, when spoken to about her supposed passion for him some years afterwards by Sir James Fellows, she ridiculed the idea, saying that she always felt for Johnson the same respect and veneration as for a Pascal. But if the long-continued manifestation of these sentiments, coupled with the most assiduous devotion and tender, wifelike care, had not awakened in him some response beyond mere gratitude, he would have been the most insensible of beings. Love, moreover, is frequently the result of propinquity and habit, and to both these influences Johnson was subjected for more than sixteen years. If he misinterpreted the attentions he received, and was emboldened by them to hope for a return of the passion they aroused, he did only what many a wise man has done under the same circumstances, and will do again.

But, while both Johnson himself and all his friends saw nothing like love in his relations with Mrs. Thrale, the outside world was convinced that it existed, and, upon Mr. Thrale's death, fully expected Dr. Johnson to marry his widow. This belief produced a number of literary squibs ridiculing the match, of which specimens are given by Boswell, and others, too coarse for reproduction, are preserved in the library of the British Museum. It is certain, at least, that he took her desertion of him very much to heart, and suffered intensely from it. Boswell, in his animosity against Mrs. Thrale, says this plainly, and descants upon the pain which her remarriage caused him. An anonymous friend, in a biography pub-

BITTER DISAPPOINTMENT.

lished the year following his death, also writes:

"No event since the decease of Mrs. Johnson so deeply affected him as the very unaccountable marriage of Mrs. Thrale. This woman he had frequently mentioned as the ornament and pattern of her sex. There was no virtue which she did not practise; no feminine accomplishment of which she was not a mistress; hardly any language or science or art which she did not know. These various endowments he considered as so many collateral securities of her worth. They conciliated his confidence, at least in what he thought she was. He consequently entertained a sincere friendship for her and her family. But her apostasy appeared to him an insult on his discernment, and on all those valuable qualities for which he had given her so much credit. The uneasiness and regret which he felt on this occasion was so very pungent that he could not conceal it even from his servants. From that time he was seldom observed to be in his usual easy good humors. His sleep and appetite, and the satisfaction he took in his study, obviously forsook him. He even avoided that company which had formerly given him the greatest pleasure. He often was denied to his dearest friends, who declined mentioning her name to him, and till the day of his death he could not wholly dismiss her from his thoughts."

Mrs. Thrale married Piozzi July 25, 1784,

and Johnson died on Dec. 13 of the same year. It would be unjust to say that his death was caused by the marriage, because he had long been the victim of a disease which must, sooner or later, be fatal. But a struggle had been going on in his mind ever since Mr. Thrale's death, April 4, 1781, or more than three years and a half. Mrs. Thrale broke up the establishment at Streatham in 1782, and in June, 1783, Johnson had a stroke of paralysis, from which, however, he recovered in a few weeks. A significant extract from his diary, under date of April 15, 1783, is transcribed by his biographer, Hawkins:

"I took leave of Mrs. Thrale. I was much moved. I had some expostulations with her. She said that she was likewise affected. I commended the Thrales with great good will to God. May my petitions have been heard!"

This proves that at this date differences had arisen between the two which could not have failed to produce an unfavorable effect upon Johnson's health. An interview between him and Madame d'Arblay, which occurred Nov. 23, 1783, is thus described by the lady:

"Nothing had yet publicly transpired with certainty or authority relative to the projects of Mrs. Thrale, who had now been nearly a year at Bath, though nothing was left unreported or unasserted with respect to her proceedings. Nevertheless, how far Dr. Johnson was himself informed, or was ignorant on the subject, neither Dr. Burney nor his daughter could tell, and each equally feared to learn.

"Scarcely an instant, however, was the latter left alone at Bolt Court ere she saw the justice of her long apprehensions, for while she planned speaking upon some topics that might have a chance to catch the attention of the Doctor, a sudden change from kind tranquillity to strong austerity took place in his altered countenance, and, startled and affrighted, she held her peace. . . .

"Thus passed a few minutes in which she scarcely dared breathe, while the respiration of the Doctor, on the contrary, was of asthmatic force and loudness; then, suddenly turning to her with an air of mingled wrath and woe, he hoarsely ejaculated, 'Piozzi!'

"He evidently meant to say more, but the effort with which he articulated that name robbed him of any voice for amplification, and his whole frame grew tremulously convulsed.

"At length, and with great agitation, he broke forth with: 'She cares for no one! You, only—

you, she loves still ! but no one—and nothing else—you she still loves—'

"A half-smile now, though of no very gay character, softened a little the severity of his features, while he tried to resume some cheerfulness in adding: 'As . . . she loves her little finger!'"

The fact was, that at this time Mrs. Thrale, so far from being about to marry Piozzi, whom she had begun to love even before her husband's death, had resolved, in deference to the opposition of her daughters and of her friends, to give him up. The struggle cost her so dear, and had, visibly, so bad an effect upon her health, that her eldest daughter became alarmed, and in May, 1784, of her own accord, begged her mother to send for her lover. He arrived on the 1st of July, after an absence of fourteen months, and as has been said, on the 25th the pair were married. She announced her intention to Johnson, among the other guardians of her children, by a circular letter dated June 30, speaking of the marriage as irrevocably settled. Johnson answered:

"MADAM,—If I interpret your letter right, you are ignominiously married. If it is yet undone, let

A BRUTAL LETTER.

us once more talk together. If you have abandoned your children and your religion, God forgive your wickedness; if you have forfeited your fame and your country, may your folly do no further mischief. If the last act is yet to do, I, who have loved you, esteemed you, reverenced you, and served you, I, who long thought you the first of womankind, entreat that before your fate is irrevocable I may once more see you. I was, I once was, madam, most truly yours,   SAM. JOHNSON.

"JULY, 2, 1784.

"I will come down if you will permit it."

To this brutal missive Mrs. Thrale replied with becoming dignity, bidding Johnson farewell until he should change his tone. Her firmness elicited the following more moderate and yet pathetic communication:

"LONDON, July 8, 1784.

"DEAR MADAM,—What you have done, however I may lament it, I have no pretence to resent, as it has not been injurious to me. I therefore breathe out one sigh more of tenderness, perhaps useless, but at least sincere.

"I wish that God may grant you every blessing, that you may be happy in this world for its short continuance, and eternally happy in a better state, and whatever I can contribute to your happiness I am very ready to repay for that kindness which soothed twenty years of a life radically wretched.

"Do not think slightly of the advice which I now presume to offer. Prevail upon Mr. Piozzi to settle in England. You may live here with more dignity than in Italy, and with more security. Your rank will be higher and your fortune more under your own eyes. I desire not to detail all my reasons, but every argument of prudence and of interest is for England, and only some phantoms of imagination seduce you to Italy.

"I am afraid, however, that my counsel is vain, yet I have eased my heart by giving it.

"When Queen Mary took the resolution of sheltering herself in England, the Archbishop of St. Andrew's, attempting to dissuade her, attended her on her journey; and when they came to the irremeable stream that separated the two kingdoms, walked by her side into the water, in the middle of which he seized her bridle, and, with earnestness proportioned to her danger and his own affection, pressed her to return. The queen went forward. If the parallel goes this far, may it go no further. The tears stand in my eyes.

"I am going into Derbyshire, and hope to be followed by your good wishes, for I am, with great affection,   Yours, &c.

"Any letters that come for me hither will be sent to me."

In a memorandum endorsed on this letter Mrs. Thrale says: "I wrote him a very kind and affectionate farewell." How keenly he felt her loss appears from the record which Madame d'Arblay makes of her last visit to him, Nov. 25, 1784, four months after Mrs. Thrale's marriage, and only nineteen days previous to his death:

"I had seen Miss Thrale the day before. 'So, said he, 'did I.' 'Did you ever, sir, hear from her mother?' 'No,' cried he, 'nor write to her. If I meet with one of her letters I burn it instantly. I have burned all I can find. I never speak of her, and I desire never to hear of her more. I drive her, as I said, wholly from my mind.'"

Contrary to Johnson's gloomy forebodings, Mrs. Thrale's marriage was eminently happy. Her new husband was of her own age, gentle in his manners, and sufficiently intellectual and accomplished to be an agreeable companion. She lived with him awhile in Italy, and then returned to London, where she was received in a friendly if not in a cordial manner. In 1795 the couple removed to Wales, and Piozzi died there in March, 1809. In 1814 Mrs. Piozzi returned to England, residing, until her death, alternately at Bath and at Clifton, with occasional visits to her old home at Streatham. When she was nearly eighty she took a fancy to an actor named Conway, who was a handsome man, six feet tall, but with little mind. Some letters are extant purporting to have been written by her to him, but their authenticity is doubtful and their contents not remarkable. On the 27th of January, 1820, she gave at Bath, to between six and seven hundred people, a concert, a ball, and a supper in celebration of her eightieth birthday, though, unless all the records are wrong, she could not on that day have been older than seventy-nine. In May, 1821, she died, having preserved her faculties to the last.

GOETHE.

GOETHE AND CHARLOTTE VON STEIN.

Among the many love affairs in which the poet Goethe was engaged during his long and brilliant career, that between him and Charlotte von Stein is distinguished by the comparatively high social rank of the lady, the depth, tenderness, and duration of her lover's affection for her, the influence it had upon him, the mystery attending its sudden interruption, and the fact that the thousand or so letters which he wrote to her during its continuance were carefully preserved by her, and since her death have been published. Recently, also, an interesting controversy took place in Germany over the nature of the relations between the pair, some writers insisting that they were criminal, but the great majority adhering to the opinion that they were perfectly pure.

Goethe first became acquainted with Frau von Stein on his arrival at Weimar towards the close of the year 1775. She was then thirty-three years of age, and had been married eleven years, during the first nine of which she had been the mother of seven children. Of these children only three sons had survived, the youngest, Fritz, who afterwards became Goethe's pet, being then three years old. Her husband, the Freiherr Friedrich von Stein, was Stallmeister, or Master of the Horse, to the Duke of Weimar. He was seven years older than his wife, and is described as a handsome, well-made man, of prepossessing appearance and manners, and a perfect courtier, but dull and unimpressionable, and almost painfully pious. His official duties kept him most of the time at court, and he even took most of his meals there, so that his wife and family saw but little of him. Charlotte herself was familiar with court life, having been for seven years previous to her marriage maid-of-honor to the duke's mother. Her husband's title of "Freiherr" is usually translated in English "baron," and hence she is called by English writers "baroness," but in Germany she is always spoken of simply as "Frau" von Stein and "Goethe's Friend" (*Goethes Freundin*). Her father, Wilhelm von Schardt, occupied in the ducal court the position of "Hofmarschall," or Intendant of the Household. On her mother's side she was of Scotch descent, being related to the Irvings of Drum, and it is worth mentioning that her younger sister, Louise, became the second wife of that Baron Imhof who accepted from Warren Hastings a large sum of money for his consent to a divorce from his first wife in order that Hastings might marry her.

Of Frau von Stein's personal appearance and characteristics our information is meagre. Goethe himself nowhere praises her beauty; and Schiller, writing in 1787, when she was near forty-five, says that she could never have had any. She suffered, moreover, greatly from ill-health, the result of a naturally weak constitution, frequent childbearing, and sorrow for the loss of all her infant daughters. Goethe wrote under her silhouette, taken in 1773, which he saw at Strasburg in the possession of the famous Dr. Zimmermann, author of the work on "Solitude," in July, 1775, some months before he made her personal acquaintance: "It were a glorious spectacle to observe how the world mirrors itself in this soul. She sees the world as it is, and yet through the medium of love. So, gentleness is the general impression." A month later he gave to the physiognomist Lavater the following analysis of the character indicated by the same silhouette: "Firmness, pleased, unchanged permanence of state, contentment in self, lovable pleasingness, naïveté, and goodness, self-flowing speech, yielding firmness, benevolence, constancy, conquers with nets." Knebel, an intimate friend of Goethe, writes of her, in a letter addressed to his sister about the same time: "She is without pretension and affectation, straightforward, natural, free, not too heavy and not too light, without enthusiasm and yet with spiritual warmth, takes an interest in all rational and human subjects, is well informed and has fine tact and even aptitude for art." Schiller, also, while denying to her the possession of beauty, calls her "a truly original, interesting person." "Her countenance," he says, "has a gentle earnestness and a very peculiar openness. Sound understanding, feeling, and truth lie in her being." Fritz von Stolberg mentions among the "lovely little women of the court" the "beautiful-eyed, lovely, gentle Stein," and speaks of her as "the beautiful Stein." Evidently her eyes and her expression made up for her physical defects, and produced at least the impression of loveliness.

Charlotte's childhood and youth, apparently, were not happy. Her mother was a mild, earnest, and deeply pious woman, devoted to her household duties. Her father was stern and hard, and, like her husband, much of the time away from home, absorbed in his official work. Her biographer, Düntzer, says that she never played with a doll, and was, as a child, fond of gazing at the stars! The means of the family were limited, and she seems to have received little education until after she became, at the age of fifteen, maid-of-honor. She then acquainted herself with French literature, learned to play the piano and the guitar, to draw, and to do various sorts of women's work. In later life she cultivated her talent for painting assiduously, and frequent references to the fruits of her skill in this art are made by Goethe in his letters. She also wrote a number of poems, a collection of which was published, set to music, and a tragedy called "Dido," which has considerable merit. To women she seems to have been especially attractive. The youthful Duchess Louise contracted with her a life-long intimacy, she deeply attached to herself Schiller's wife, and the companions of her old age spoke of her with affectionate tenderness. It is related that Knebel, Goethe's friend, was so affected by her death that he wept like a child.

When Goethe arrived at Weimar he was a little more than twenty-six years old. His literary reputation had been established by the publication of "Götz von Berlichingen," the "Sorrows of Werther," "Clavigo," "Stella," "Erwin and Elmira," and countless little poems. Personally he was of almost god-like beauty. Lewes, in his biography, says of him that, at twenty, when he entered a restaurant, people laid down their knives and forks to look at him. His features resembled those of the Vatican Apollo; he was above the middle height, strong, quick in his movements, and versed in all kinds of manly exercises. Of his appearance when he was twenty-five, skating on the ice at Frankfort, wrapped in a crimson cloak, his delighted mother said: "Anything so beautiful is not to be seen now. I clapped my hands for joy. Never shall I forget him, as he darted out from under one arch of the bridge and in again under the other, the wind carrying the train behind him as he flew!" This personal beauty he retained till his death, and his friend Eckermann says of his corpse as it lay stretched out for burial: "I was astonished at the god-like splendor of his limbs. The breast, above all, mighty, broad, and arched. Arms and thighs full and gently muscular, the feet elegant and of the purest shape, and nowhere in the whole body a trace either of fat or leanness and falling away. A perfect man lay in great beauty before me, and the delight that it gave me made me for a moment forget that the immortal soul had departed from such an envelope." Nor were his powers of pleasing inferior to his physical attractions. If his successes with women were not enough to prove this, we have the favorable impression which he made not only upon his patron, the Duke of Weimar, but upon the whole court. The enthusiastic friendships which he aroused in men also attest in him the possession of that most desirable of all qualities, the ability to bind the hearts of others to one's own.

It was not without reason, therefore, that Dr. Zimmermann warned Frau von Stein against the fascinations of this handsome young genius. The doctor had attended her at the baths of Pyrmont in 1773, and obtained from her there the silhouette which he showed to Goethe in 1775, and the sight of which, he assured her, had cost Goethe three sleepless nights. She, in return, having expressed a wish to make Goethe's acquaintance, the doctor wrote to her: "But, my poor friend, you do not reflect. You desire to see him, and you do not know how dangerous to you this lovable and charming man may become." Goethe's loves had been notorious, and his engagement to Anna Schönemann (Lili) which had just then been broken off, was only the last of a series of like affairs which began when he was but fifteen years of age. But his sweethearts had all been of his own citizen rank. Gretchen, the first, was scarcely respectable, Katharina Schönkopf was the daughter of a tavern-keeper, and Charity Meixner of a merchant in Worms. Then followed his entanglement with his dancing-master's daughter, and next, that with Frederika Brion, the daughter of the pastor of Sesenheim. In Wetzlar he fell in love with Charlotte Buff, the original of Werther's Charlotte, who was the daughter of a law official. Next came Maximiliane Laroche, afterwards Madame Brentano, whose father and husband were both merchants. Anna Sybilla Münch was of a Frankfort citizen family, and Lili, whom he came so near to marrying, had a rich banker for father. In Frau von Stein he loved for the first time in his life a woman of the world and a lady of rank. Her birth, her connections, her training, and her manners were all superior to those of the women to whom he had been accustomed, and must have impressed his artistic sense with a new idea of femininity. It is difficult for us Americans to conceive of the gulf which existed in Germany a century ago, and which has not yet been obliterated, between patricians and plebeians, the noble and the citizen. It was not merely a matter of birth and position, but one of breeding, manners, and habits. Goethe himself was conscious of his deficiencies in this respect, and took great pains to repair them. So late as 1782, when he had been six years living at court in Weimar, he writes to Frau von Stein, who had undertaken to form him: "I strive after all that we last discussed concerning conduct, life, demeanor, and elegance, let myself go, am always attentive, and I can assure you that all whom I observe play more their own parts than I do mine." Two years later he makes Wilhelm Meister* discuss the dif-

* *Lehrjahre*, Book V., chap. 3.

ference between citizens and nobles in a way which evidently expresses his own ideas on the subject. "I know not how it is in foreign lands, but in Germany only to a nobleman is a certain universal, so to speak, personal education possible. A citizen may gain merit for himself and at most educate his mind, but his personality is lost, present himself as he will, whereas it is the duty of a nobleman, who deals with the elegant, to give himself an elegant demeanor, while this demeanor, since no door is shut to him, becomes free, and, since he must pay with his figure and with his person, be it in the court or in the army, he has a reason for thinking something of himself, and for showing that he thinks something of himself." Indeed, although early ennobled by patent, Goethe, to the end of his life, never became a thorough patrician. The etiquette of the Weimar court, the observance of which to Frau von Stein was second nature, wearied him immensely. He hated the entertainments which he was obliged to attend, and was irritated because his beloved took pleasure in them and was gracious and complaisant to the men she met at them. His great delight was to steal off from time to time to Jena, and there join in revelry with the students, and, as we shall see hereafter, his coarseness in dealing with women ultimately led to a breach between him and the object of his adoration.

Precisely when and where Goethe first met Frau von Stein face to face does not anywhere appear, nor is it known what impression each then made upon the other. Goethe reached Weimar Nov. 7, 1775, and the records of the court make no mention of Frau von Stein at any of the entertainments at which he was present about that time. She was, however, well acquainted with the family of which he was the guest, and that within a month he paid her a visit at her husband's country-seat, Kochberg, appears from an inscription on a writing-table still preserved there, "Goethe den 6 Dcbr. 75." Ten years later he reminded his beloved of this first visit in a letter written on the same spot: "I think of thee, my love, in the old castle, where, ten years ago, I first visited thee, and where

CHARLOTTE'S FASCINATIONS. 89

thou heldest me so fast through thy love." This indicates that even at that time he was enamoured of his new acquaintance, and then, or very soon thereafter, began the romance in action between the pair which is the most remarkable in Goethe's career. He had just broken off his engagement with Lili, and his susceptible heart abhorred a vacuum. He was therefore prepared for the installation of a new idol, and he found one in Frau von Stein. He had come to Weimar for a visit to the young duke of only a few weeks, but her fascinations kept him there, first, during the winter, then for another year, until finally he became a permanent resident of the place and died in it. Indeed, he repeatedly says, as he does in the letter just above quoted, that Frau von Stein was the tie which held him, and but for which he would have soon departed.

The ten years and eight months which elapsed between Goethe's first acquaintance with Frau von Stein at the end of 1775, and his departure for Italy in September, 1786, may be called the golden period of their intercourse. Of his 965 published letters to her, 821 were written during this period, and, as the few extracts hereafter given will show, they embody the most ardent emotions of which a lover's soul is capable. It is, indeed, comforting to ordinary men, who are aware that, at some time or other in their lives, love has made fools of them, to find that a great genius like Goethe was also the victim of the same and even greater madness. What the letters fail to exhibit, however, is the gentle, refining influence which Frau von Stein exercised upon her lover. It was under the sway of his intercourse with her that he wrote his "Iphigenia," "Tasso," "Egmont," and the first part of "Wilhelm Meister," besides a number of graceful little plays and spectacles for the Weimar theatre, and many dainty short poems, like the "Wanderer's Night Song" and "Ueber alle Gipfel," which are printed with the letters. In her companionship, also, he practised drawing and painting, studied English, Dutch, and Italian, and experimented with the microscope. Her children were frequent visitors at his house. He played with them, told them stories, and sometimes kept them with him overnight. The youngest, Fritz, he, in a manner, adopted, took him with him on his journeys to the neighboring towns, helped to educate him, and, finally, established him in an official position. His letters indicate that his visits to her, except when interrupted by her absence from Weimar or his own, were made almost daily, and that she, in turn, visited him as often. In short, there was between the two that freedom of thought and complete confidence which is the ideal of friendship, if not of love.

By the end of December, 1775, or early in January, 1776, Goethe began to pour out his feelings to Frau von Stein in the long series of letters of which mention has been made. As he jokingly warned her at the outset: "If this goes on thus from morning to night there will be a perfect disease of notes between us." Some days he wrote to her morning, noon, and night, and the average of the letters for ten years is one in four days. It is much to be regretted that the corresponding letters from Frau von Stein to him no longer exist, but, shortly before her death, she made him return them to her, and remorselessly destroyed them, together with the autograph manuscripts of a number of poems which he had sent her. There is a pretty legend that Goethe retained one of her notes, burned it, and preserved the ashes as a memorial, but this is unsupported by evidence. She, on her part, carefully kept his letters to her, and they are now in the possession of her descendants. The first edition of them appeared about 1850, and a second, in two large octavo volumes, corrected and improved, and enriched with a mass of valuable notes, was published in 1883.

The total number of the letters in the manuscript collection is 1624, including some from others than Goethe. Those published are numbered up to 965. The originals are described by the editor as being mostly on paper of letter and of note size of various colors, with printed borders, and written partly in ink and partly in pencil. Others are on leaves torn out of note books, and on scraps evidently caught up in haste from the desk or table at which Goethe was sitting, engaged in his official duties. Many of them were sent unsealed, and carelessly folded, as if there was no desire to conceal their contents. Some of them bear no date, and, although Frau von Stein had put them in order, yet, during the plunder of her house by the French in 1806, they were mixed up, and now their true succession is in many cases a matter of conjecture. Still, by patient labor and research, an arrangement of them has been made which for practical purposes is sufficient.

Unromantically enough, the very first of the letters, presumably written early in January, 1776, begins with thanks for the gift of—a sausage! and details of a hurt to Goethe's eye, caused by the blow of a whip lash. Likewise, all through the letters frequent mention is made of presents of fruit, vegetables, game, and even cooked dishes, with an abundance of details respecting the bodily health of both the lovers. The next letter is more sentimental, and the next, dated Jan. 15, begins: "I am glad that I am coming away, to wean myself from you." Other like expressions indicate a passion that had already reached a high pitch. A day or two after this he calls Charlotte his "soother" (*Besänftigerin*). By the 28th of January he became bolder:

"DEAR ANGEL,—I shall not come to the concert, for I am so well that I cannot see people. Dear angel, I sent for my letters, and it vexed me that there was not among them one word from thee, not even in pencil—no good-night. Dear lady, suffer it that I hold thee so dear. If I can love any one more, I will tell thee, will leave thee in peace. Adieu, Gold, thou comprehendest not how I love thee."

It will be observed that in this letter Goethe drops from the formal "you" into the familiar "thou," a liberty in Germany, as in France and Italy, permissible only to an intimate friend. On Feb. 12 he addresses to his lady-love his "Wanderer's Night Song," which closes with the words, "Sweet peace, come, oh, come, into my heart!" This little poem Frau von Stein must have shown to her mother, for on the back of it are written in that pious lady's hand these words from the Gospel of St. John: "Peace I leave with you, my peace I give unto you. Not as the world giveth give I unto you. Let not your heart be troubled, neither let it be afraid." Frau von Stein herself, also, from first to last exhibited a religious turn of mind. She went to church regularly every Sunday, and, although neglected by her husband and sorely pressed by her impetuous young lover, she never for a moment, except perhaps at the very last, faltered in the observance of her wifely obligations. She seems even at times to have regarded her acceptance of Goethe's devotion as a sin, and, as we shall see further on, speaks of it as such.

Towards the end of February Goethe writes: "O, that my sister had a brother such as I in thee have a sister! Think of me, and press thy hand to thy lips, for thou will never wean Gusteln from his naughtiness, which will only end with his unrest and love in the grave." A month later he says: "I see well, dear lady, when one loves thee it is as if seed were sown, and springs unnoticed, unfolds and stands there—and God give his blessing to it. Amen!"

On the 14th of April Goethe sends a long poem, in which occur the lines:

> "Ah! thou wert in a former life
> Either my sister or my wife."

And again, on the 16th, he writes: "Adieu, dear sister, since so it must be." Evidently Frau von Stein had sought to repress the ardor of her young admirer, and, as other women have tried to do in like circumstances, to keep his passion within the bounds of a sisterly affection. As usual, too, she failed at an early stage of the game. On May 1 her lover breaks out with: "To-day will I not see you. Your presence yesterday made such a wonderful impression on me that I do not know whether it be weal or woe with me in the affair. Farewell, dearest lady."

Failing to check him otherwise, Frau von Stein must soon after this have appealed to his regard for her reputation, and have begged him to consider what the world would say of his attentions. In reply he writes May 24, falling back partially into the formal "you:"

"And so, a relation, the purest, the most beautiful, the truest that I have ever had with any woman, except my sister, that also is interrupted! I was prepared for it. I suffered infinitely for the past and the future, and for the poor child who went forth, and whom I devoted that moment to such suffering. I will not see you. Your presence would make me sad. If I cannot live with you, your love helps me as little as the love of my absent ones in which I am so rich. Presence in the moment of need decides all, assuages all, strengthens all. The absent comes with his fire hose when the fire is under. And all that on account of the world. The world, which can be nothing to me, will not allow thee to be anything to me. You do not know what you do. The hand of the lonely prisoner, who hears not the voice of love, presses hard where it rests. Adieu, best one."

To this passionate outburst she must have replied soothingly, for the next day he writes: "You are always the same, always endless love and goodness. Forgive that I make you suffer. I will hereafter strive to learn to bear it alone." On the 1st of June he becomes sarcastic. "I am here again, and have come as willingly as I live—but it must not be—my absence will have consoled the world somewhat."

For some weeks after this things ran on smoothly, and the letters indicate more tranquillity in the writer. July 9 he says:

"Last night I lay in bed half asleep. Philip [his servant] brought me a letter. I read it in a doze—that Lilli is betrothed! turned over and slept on. How I prayed destiny to deal so with me! So all in good time. Dear angel, good-night."

Early in September his beloved seems to have been again obliged to repress his demonstrations, and again he bursts out:

"Why shall I plague thee, dearest creature? Why cheat myself and plague thee, and so on? We can be nothing to one another, and are too much to one another. Believe me, if I spoke as plain as a string, thou art at one with me in all. But just because I see things as they are, that makes me wild. Good-night, angel, and good-morning. I will not see thee again. Only—thou knowest all—I have my heart. It is all stupid what I could say. I see thee henceforth as one sees a star. Think on that."

A little later he writes: "You have a

CHARLOTTE VON STEIN.

way of giving pain, as fate has. One cannot complain of it, however much it hurts." Again, on the 7th of October, he utters this passionate cry:

"Farewell, best one! You go, and God knows what will happen. I ought to have been thankful to Fate, which let me clearly feel the first moment I saw you again how dear I held you. I ought to have been satisfied with it and never have seen you more. Forgive me; I see now how my presence plagues you; how pleasing it is to me that you go. In the same city I cannot endure it. Yesterday I brought you flowers and peaches, but could not give them to you as you were, and so I gave them to your sister. You seem to me at times like the Madonna ascending to heaven. In vain the bereaved one stretches out his arms to her; in vain his piercing, tearful sight wishes his own down again, she has vanished in the glory which surrounds her, full of eagerness for the crown which floats over her head. Yet, adieu, my love."

Frau von Stein, touched by this despairing appeal, and apparently conscious of the impression which her ardent young lover had made upon her heart, wrote on the back of the paper the following lines:

"Whether what I feel be wrong,
And if I must expiate my sin so dear,
My conscience will not say to me,
Cancel it, thou, O Heaven! if ever it accuses me."

After this the intercourse between the pair seems to have settled down into a quiet, confidential friendship, which lasted many months. Goethe's letters contain frequent inquiries after his beloved's health, written mostly on rising in the morning and going to bed at night, with information concerning his own condition and feelings, besides references to his literary work.

In the winter of 1777-8, Goethe made an expedition into the Harz Mountains, during which he wrote almost daily to Frau von Stein. In September, 1779, he went on a trip to Switzerland, and on the way stopped at Sesenheim, where he saw again his old love Frederika Brion, the pastor's daughter. He writes a full account of the interview to Frau von Stein, and assures her, as he did Frederika, that no trace of his former passion remained in his heart. The rest of 1779 he devoted to the Swiss tour, sending a full narrative of it to Frau von Stein in letters which he afterwards worked over and published under the title "Letters from Switzerland." After returning to Weimar he resumed the customary tenor of his life, but it was again disturbed by outbreaks of wild longing. Thus, June 24, 1780, he writes:

"From my unutterable desire to see you again I just begin to feel how I love you. Things hang wonderfully together in men. This craving for you hits exactly the nerve where the old pain, caused by not seeing you in Kochberg the first year, had healed itself; brings the very sensation forth, and reminds me, like an old melody, of that time."

Some time in September, 1780, he gave vent to his feelings in the beautiful song commencing "Ueber alle Gipfel findest du Ruh," which Frau von Stein copied on the back of one of his letters. In October we find him breaking out once more into a passionate complaint, almost untranslatable into English, so confused and involved is its language:

"What you last said to me early this morning has pained me deeply, and if the duke had not gone with me up the mountain I should have wept bitterly. One trouble follows another. Yes; it is a rage against one's own flesh, when an unhappy one, to get air for himself, strives through it to injure his dearest, and, if it were only a paroxysm of temper and I could be conscious of it! But I am by my thousand thoughts so reduced again to a child, unacquainted with the moment, doubtful of myself, that I consume the belongings of another as with a blazing fire.

"I shall never give myself peace until you render me a verbal account of the past, and for the future endeavor to persuade yourself into so sisterly a state that nothing of the kind can again affect it. Otherwise, I must avoid you in the very moments when I have most need of you. It seems horrible to me to spoil the best hours of life, the moments of our companionship; with you, for whom I would willingly pull every hair from my head, if I could change it into a pleasure, and yet to be so blind, so dumb! Have pity on me! That all came to the state of my soul, in which it seemed a pandemonium filled with invisible spirits, and to the spectator, fearful as he was, presented only an infinite, empty vault."

A day or two afterwards he writes: "It is wonderful, and yet it is so, that I am jealous and stupid, like a boy, when you meet others in a friendly manner," which may possibly indicate that his trouble was caused by her favorable treatment of some other admirer.

The following months exhibit a peaceful record, and how sweet and soothing her influence upon him was, during this period, appears from the concluding paragraph of a long letter written by him from Neunheiligen, March 11, 1781:

"Adieu, sweet support of my inmost heart. I see and hear nothing good that I do not at the same moment share with thee. And all my observations of the world, and of myself, direct themselves, like Mark Antony, not to my own, but to my second self. By means of this dialogue, in which, in respect of everything, I think what you would say to it, all becomes brighter and worthier to me."

The next day he continues the strain:

"My soul has grown fast to thine. I will make no word. Thou knowest that I am inseparable from thee, and that neither height nor depth can sunder me from thee. I would that there were some vow or sacrament that would make me thine, visibly and lawfully. What would it be worth to me! And my novitiate has been long enough to make it worth thinking of. I can no longer write 'you,' as I could not for a long time say 'thou.'

"On my knees I beg thee to end thy work and to make me quite good. Thou canst, not only if thou lovest me; but thy power is infinitely increased when thou knowest that I love thee. Farewell."

March 22, he writes:

"Thy love is like the morning and the evening star—it sets after the sun and rises before it. Rather, it is like the pole star, which never sets, and which weaves over our heads an ever-living garland. I pray that the gods may never dim it for me over the path of my life."

On the 27th of March:

"The openness and peace of my heart which thou hast again given me be for thee alone, and all good to others and to myself which springs from it be also thine. Believe me, I feel quite changed; my old benevolence comes back, and with it the joy of my life. Thou hast given me delight in good, which I had quite lost."

Again, April 22:

"Last night I had a great mind to throw my ring into the water, like Polycrates, for I counted up my happiness in the stillness and found a monstrous sum."

May 30, he says: "My heart hath hid

nothing from thine, and when I conceal faults from thee it is in order not to distress thy love." Again, Oct. 29: "Thy love is the beauteous light of all my days, thy applause my best renown, and if I prize a good name abroad it is for thy sake, that I may not shame thee."

Later, this feeling swelled to a state resembling ecstasy, as the following extracts will show

"Feb. 11, 1782.—Say one word to me, Lotte. It is with me in thy love, as if I dwelt no longer in tents and huts, but as if I had received the gift of a well-founded house in which to live and die and keep all my possessions. Before ten I will see thee a moment. I cannot say farewell, for I never leave thee."

"March 20.—O, thou best one! All my life I have had an ideal wish how I would fain be loved, and have ever sought its fulfilment in vain in dreams of fancy. Now that the world daily becomes brighter to me, I find it at last in thee, in a manner that I never can lose it."

"March 22.—Farewell, dear life. When thou writest me that thou hast slept well, it gives me new strength for the whole day. God keep thee. Since I have had in thy love rest and an abiding place, the world is so bright and so dear to me! Among people I name thy name silently to myself, and I live away from thee only for thy sake."

"April 9.—Over thy last letter I have had many sad thoughts, and one night I wept bitterly as I figured to myself that I might lose thee. Against all which can probably happen to me I have a counterpoise in myself, but against this one thing nothing. Hope helps us to live, and I think again thou art well and will be well when thou receivest this."

"May 12.—Thou hast set in my eyes and in my ears little sprites who from all that I see and hear exact a tribute of reverence for thee."

"June 5.—Tell me, my best, if thou art well. I have no joyous hour so long as thou art ill."

The month of July, 1782, seems to have been troubled by a lovers' quarrel, the nature of which does not appear. The references to it in the letters are these:

"July 19.—Tell me, dear Lotte, how wert thou on getting up. Tell me, is it physical, or hast thou something on thy soul which makes thee ill? Thou dost not believe how thy condition yesterday pained me. The only interest of my life is that you should be open with me. I cannot endure reserve."

"July 22.—I will not be troublesome, but only say this much, that I have not deserved it. That I feel, and keep silence."

"July 23.—So, thank God, it was a misunderstanding that led thee to write thy note. I am still stunned by it. It was like death. There is only one word and no idea for such a thing."

"July 24.—I hope it will be so, yet I sit and look before me. It is like a void in my whole being. A thousand thanks for thy love. I cannot collect myself. Do not worry. Thou canst do anything. Oh, beloved, I will come as soon as I can."

"July 25.—I slept long and well; thy early message has been received, and is the first greeting of the new day. I am a deal better, yet feel lame, like one struck by lightning, but this will soon pass off if the one medicine is employed. When I think of it I shudder again, and I shall never rest until I am safe for the future."

Then came another tranquil period:

"Aug. 23.—Whatever I write to thee, my pen will say only, I love! I love!"

"Aug. 24.—Thou knowest, Lotte, how I love thee. Thanks for thy note. Good-night. My thoughts never leave thee."

"Aug. 25.—At last I get thy leaflet. O, thou love! I believe and feel that I am ever in thy presence."

"Nov. 17.—I roamed over my deserted house as Melusina did over hers, to which she was not to return, and I thought of the past, of which I understand nothing, and of the future, of which I know nothing. How much I have lost since I had to leave that quiet abode! It was the second tie that held me; now I hang on thee alone, and, thank God, this is the strongest. For some days I have been looking over the letters which have been written to me the last ten years, and I comprehend less and less what I am and what I ought to be.

"Abide with me, dear Lotte, thou art my anchor between these reefs."

"Nov. 21.—Farewell, thou sweet dream of my life, thou anodyne of my sorrows."

"Nov. 28.—I wish to be only where thou art, for where thou art there is my heaven."

"Dec. 26.—Adieu, my inmost beloved, to whom I turn all my thoughts, to whom I refer everything."

"Dec. 29.—O, dear Lotte, I am indebted to thee for my happiness at home and my pleasure abroad. The peace, the equanimity with which I accept and give, rests on the foundation of thy love."

"April 8, 1783.—Farewell, thou sweet joy of my life, thou only desire of my whole being."

"April 16.—How I think of thee, how present thou art to me, how thy love guides me like a familiar star, I will not tell thee. I would not increase my longing while I write to thee. The skies brighten, and I hope for some good days. I am busy and employ myself with earthly things on earthly accounts. My inner life is with thee, and my kingdom not of this world. Adieu, best one."

Here are some musical illustrations, of various dates :

"Thou art heartily good and dear, and yet thou canst not do too much. For, only a breath, only a sound which comes over from thee to me, out of tune, changes the whole atmosphere around me."

"As music is nothing without the human voice, so would my life be nothing without thy love."

"As a sweet melody lifts us on high, and forms under our cares and sorrow a soft cloud, so is to me thy being and thy love."

"The very sight of the Imhof [Charlotte's sister] gave me pain. She is like the seventh, which makes the ear long for the chord."

About the beginning of May, 1783, the

serenity of the poet's mind seems to have been again troubled by some occurrence which, owing to the loss of Frau von Stein's letters, cannot be now explained. May 4 he writes:

"The way in which thou saidst to me yesterday evening that thou hadst a story to tell me worried me a moment. I feared it was something referring to our love, and I know not why. I have been for some time in anxiety. How wonderful that the entire weight of one's happiness should hang on a single thread like this."

Peace seems to have been restored to him soon after, and he writes:

"July 3.—The memory of thy love is ever with me, and my inclination to thee, like the fear of God, is the beginning of wisdom."

"Sept. 9.—I wish you could be with me all day invisibly, and in the evening when I am alone step forth out of the wall. Thou wouldst feel what I feel with so much joy, that I am and can be thine alone. How I hope to see thee again a moment. Thou hast bound me to thee with every bond."

This happy state continued to the end of 1783 and through the first half of 1784:

"Jan. 24, 1784.—Yesterday evening I sat up late, and restrained my longing to be with thee. I thank thee that thou dost possess so much love for me. It is my best fortune."

"March 8.—Surely thou must have thought of me on awaking as I did on thee, for such a love cannot be one-sided."

"June 5.—Since I am away from thee I have no object in life. I know not what use to make of a day when I do not see thee. It pains me most when I enjoy something good without sharing it with thee."

"June 12.—I would like to talk to thee always only of my love. How lonely I am words cannot express. I see nobody, and when I see anybody I see only one form before me in the company."

"June 17.—I continually feel my nearness to thee, thy presence never leaves me. In thee I have a standard for all women, yea, for all human beings, and in thy love a standard for every lot. Not that it makes the rest of the world seem dark, it rather brightens it. I see right plainly what people are, what they wish to think, do, and enjoy. I grant them what is theirs, and delight myself secretly in comparing my possession of so indestructible a treasure."

"June 28.—Yes, dear Lotte, now is it first plain

how thou hast become and remainest my own half. I am no individual, independent being. All my weaknesses have I hung upon thee, have protected my vulnerable points by thee, have supplied by thee all my defects. When I am far from thee my condition is a strange one. On one side I am armored and weaponed, on the other like a raw egg, for I have neglected to harness myself where thou art shield and shelter. I delight in belonging entirely to thee, and in soon seeing thee again. I love everything about thee, and everything makes me love thee more."

In August, 1784, Goethe accompanied the duke on a short visit to Brunswick; and as French was the language used at that court, his beloved imposed on him the task of writing to her in that language. He obeyed reluctantly, saying that he could not bring himself to express his true sentiments in a foreign tongue. "Nevertheless," he says, "I will persevere, for if I ever learn that language which every one thinks he knows, it will be by thee, and I shall take pleasure in owing to thee this talent, as I owe thee so many things worth much more." A dozen long letters in French were the result, and in the course of them he says:

"Aug. 21.—Ah, my only friend, dear confidante of all my thoughts, how I feel the need of talking to thee and communicating all my reflections! Thou hast isolated me in the world. I have nothing to say to anybody. I talk, not to be silent, and that is all."

"Aug. 30.—No! My love for thee is no longer a passion; it is a disease—a disease dearer to me than the most perfect health, and of which I wish not to be cured."

This characterization of love as a disease has been adopted by Stendhal in his "L'Amour," and he is generally supposed to have originated it.

The letters continue in a strain of intense devotion all through 1785 and the first half of 1786. Goethe was busy with his official duties, with his literary work, and with superintending the theatrical entertainments of the court. June 25, 1786, he writes: "Do, my love, whatever seems best, and it will be so to me also. Keep only love for me, and let us at least preserve a good which we shall never find again, although there be moments when we cannot enjoy it." In August he spent a fortnight with his beloved at Carlsbad, in the same house with her, and accompanied her to Schneeberg, returning alone to Carlsbad. From this place he departed suddenly and secretly for Italy on Sept. 3, under an assumed name, and Frau von Stein did not hear again from him until she got his letter from Verona dated Sept. 18.

Endless speculation, in the absence of positive knowledge, is, of course, possible as to the causes which led to this sudden interruption of the lovers' relations. Among others the celebrated critic, Adolf Stahr, insists that it resulted from Frau von Stein's tyranny. A review of Goethe's letters which he wrote upon their appearance in 1851, he heads with this quotation from "Vanity Fair:" "She did not wish to marry him, but she wished to keep him. She wished to give him nothing, but that he should give her all: a bargain not infrequently levied in love," and he goes on to intimate that Goethe, like Dobbin, finally became impatient of the yoke which Frau von Stein had imposed upon him:

"It was not Goethe's fault that his love for Frau von Stein did not find its natural and reasonable re-

sult and conclusion. From the very first, he sought
and strove for this only true moral conclusion with
all his strength. Charlotte von Stein ought to have
been his wife, the sole companion of his entire existence. That she did not bring herself to this,
that the strength of her love was not equal to what,
in her case, the duty of true morality commanded,
was, if she shared Goethe's love in full measure,
either a weakness of character, which set form above
substance, worldly appearance above the essence of
morality, or it was a sin against her lover. It was a
sin if her soul entirely belonged to him, and not less
a sin if, as it seems to me, she wanted to be at once
the virtuous spouse of an unloved and insignificant
husband, and the beloved, the soul-friend, the queen
of the greatest genius of his time. It was a sin also
against his future, against his destiny, against his
happiness, against the happiness which he so ardently desired, and which he knew, like few, how
to appreciate ; against the happiness which the possession of a home and a family assures in marriage.
If Goethe's development here exhibits a gap, his fate
here a dark place, yea, in his later career a heart-
breaking tragedy, a portion of the blame can never
be removed from a woman who was too petty for
the fortune which the favor of destiny offered her in
preference to so many thousands."

This means—if it means anything—that
Frau von Stein ought to have obtained a

divorce from her husband, and to have married Goethe, as the first wife of Baron Imhof was divorced from him and married to Warren Hastings! With notable inconsistency the same critic a few years later advanced the opinion that Frau von Stein had all the while maintained criminal relations with Goethe, and, as has been said, a controversy thereupon sprang up, in which several prominent writers took part. Unless we mistake greatly, the reader who has paid attention to the facts which have been presented and has perused the extracts given from Goethe's letters will have no difficulty in coming to a conclusion entirely acquitting both him and his beloved of the offence imputed to them. If direct testimony were needed, that of Schiller ought to be decisive, and he, writing from Weimar in 1787, the year after Goethe's departure for Italy, says of Frau von Stein: "This lady possesses over a thousand letters from Goethe, and he has written to her from Italy every week. They say that their intercourse (*umgang*) is entirely pure and blameless."

This being the verdict, on the spot and at the time, of a little gossipy town like Weimar, where everybody knew everything about everybody else, it is idle to seek to reverse it at this late day. Certainly the letters of Goethe express the feelings, not of a triumphant seducer, but of a humble and unsuccessful suppliant, and show that the object of his passion, so far from yielding to it, checked and resisted it to the utmost.

In confirmation of this view, it may be further remarked that up to the commencement of his acquaintance with Frau von Stein all Goethe's love affairs, so far as anything is known of them, had been purely romantic. Women loved him devotedly, but he never took advantage of their love to do them a wrong. Nearly all of them married, as Lili did, respectable husbands, which could not have been the case if they had fallen from virtue. To suppose that a lady in Frau von Stein's position should have been Goethe's first victim is to violate all probability. The fact that, subsequently, Christiane Vulpius became his mistress, proves nothing, since he always treated her as his wife, and finally married her in due legal form.

The truth, probably, is that the love of Frau von Stein for Goethe, sincere as it may have been, was not that which a woman should feel for a man with whom she is to hold wifely relations. She was seven years his senior. His youth and beauty aroused her maternal instincts, his devotion flattered her vanity, and, proud of his genius and his reputation, she was willing to have her name linked with his in public fame. Goethe, on his part, saw her "through the medium of love." His fervid imagination, like that of all lovers, invested her with charms of his own creation, and the disenchantment which finally came would have come earlier if she had yielded herself to him. De Musset is right when he says, "La femme qui aime un peu, et qui résiste, n'aime pas assez," but he is not right when he adds, "et celle qui aime assez et qui résiste, sait qu'elle est moins aimée." Love, like gratitude, is a lively sense of favors expected. It is but a step from satisfaction to satiety, and satiety is the grave of love.

Whether she loved little or much, Frau von Stein, if she had not resisted Goethe, would not only have been loved less by him, but soon would not have been loved at all. That she did that which Stahr blames her for doing was the reason why she kept her lover's affection so long, and if she had not done it his character would never have been refined and improved as it was.

It is, nevertheless, possible, but, as the hypothesis has never before been advanced by any one who has written upon the subject, it is submitted here with diffidence, that Frau von Stein, worn out with Goethe's importunities, or perhaps, yielding to the passion which his ardent devotion kindled in her heart, had, during his stay with her in Carlsbad in August, 1786, consented to fly with him to Italy, and there spend the rest of her days with him. At the last moment, however, she repented of her promise, and refused to keep it. Goethe, none the less loving her, would not and did not change his plans, and, since she would not accompany him, he went without her. It was an act of revolt against her on his part, which she felt to be the beginning of his emancipation from her influence, as, in fact, it was. Hence her grief at his going, and hence the accepted opinion that his projected journey was as much a secret to her as it was to the rest of the world. But she knew of his plans and was informed by him of his intended departure. It was no surprise to her, and the pain it caused her arose not from his want of confidence, but from the fact that he left her at all.

The proof that Goethe once expected Frau von Stein to accompany him to Italy is found in his letter to her dated at Carlsbad, Aug. 23, 1786, which, in the collection as originally published, is the last written before he went away. In this letter the following passage occurs:

"In any event, I must stay another week, but then, also, all will gently come to an end and the fruit fall ripe. And then will I live with thee in the free world, and, in happy solitude, without name and rank, come nearer to the earth out of which we were taken."

The obvious meaning of this language is that Frau von Stein was to go with Goethe.

In his previous letters he had frequently, as we have seen, expressed his overwhelming desire to have her with him constantly, and he again and again laments the necessity of being separated from her even for a few days. It is true that he made his preparations for the journey to Italy with great secrecy and started upon it under an assumed name. But that Frau von Stein did not know that he was going, letters from Goethe to her, first published by the Goethe Gesellschaft in 1886, show to be an error. These letters appear to have been sent back to Goethe along with the rest of his letters from Italy to enable him to make up his "Italian Journey," and thus were not printed with the others. In that dated Aug. 30, 1786, a week after the letter last above mentioned, he wrote from Carlsbad:

"Now, dearest, the end approaches. Sunday, the 3d September, I think I shall get away from here.

"When shall I hear from thee again? I am thine with my whole soul, and enjoy life only in thee. From here I will write once again."

On Sept. 1 he writes from the same place:

"Yet one more farewell from Carlsbad. Mrs. Waldner will bring this with her. Of all that she can tell, I say nothing, but I repeat to thee that I love thee heartily, that our last journey to Schneeberg made me right happy, and that only thy assurance that joy comes to thee from my love can bring joy to my life. I have hitherto borne much in silence, *and have desired nothing so longingly as that our relation may put itself upon such a footing that no power can affect it. Else I will not dwell near thee, and will rather remain lonely in the world into which I am now going forth.* If I am not out in my calculation, thou canst, by the end of September, secure a roll of drawings from me, but which thou must show to no one in the world. Then shalt thou learn whither thou canst write to me.

"Thou shalt soon hear from me. Adieu."

Finally, on Sept. 2, he writes:

"At last, at last, I am ready, and yet not ready, for properly I have eight days' work to do here, but I will away, and say to thee once more adieu! Farewell, thou sweet heart. I am thine.

"Night. To-morrow, Sunday, Sept. 3, I go from here. No one knows it yet; no one guesses my departure to be so near."

These same letters contain instructions to Frau von Stein respecting the use of those which he was to write to her from

Italy and of the diary of his travels which he promised to send to her from time to time. That he had no idea of escaping from her is shown by his first letter from Italy dated at Verona, Sept. 18:

"On a little leaflet give I my beloved a sign of life, without yet telling her where I am. I am well, and wish to share with thee every good that I enjoy, a wish which often comes over me with longing.

"Tell nobody anything of what you receive. It is for the present for thee alone.

"Greet me Fritz. It troubles me often that he is not with me. Had I known what I now know I had brought him with me."

From Venice, in October, he writes in a similar strain, and then, in the original published collection, we find the following, dated at Terni, Oct. 27:

"Again sitting in a cavern which a year ago suffered an earthquake, I direct my prayer to thee, my dear guardian angel. I feel now for the first time how spoiled I have been living ten years with thee, loved by thee, and now in a strange world. I foresaw it, and only the highest necessity could compel me to make the decision.

"*Let us have no other thought than to end our lives together.*"

This last sentence indicates that he had not yet given up hope of persuading his beloved to link herself to him permanently, and in all the other letters which he wrote to her from Italy similar expressions of devotion abound.

But Goethe, as Frau von Stein seems to have felt, had, unconsciously to himself, entered upon an experience which was destined to produce a fundamental revolution in his character, and to break up forever his tender relations with her. His stay in Italy, which was originally intended to last only six months, was prolonged to a year, and finally to nearly two years. He visited picture-galleries, palaces, and cities, he studied art, music, and science, he became acquainted with distinguished men and women, and, what was more destructive than anything else to Frau von Stein's dominion over him, he fell desperately in love with a pretty girl from Milan. When, therefore, in June, 1788, he returned to Weimar, he was no longer the same Goethe that he was when he went away. His twenty-two months of absence had done the work of many years. His friends noticed the change, and, as was natural, he thought it had taken place in them. Frau von Stein especially, who during his absence had been saddened by the death of her son Ernest, he reproached with receiving him coldly, and he was particularly offended because she refused to listen to the revelations which, with a singular want of delicacy, he offered to make her concerning his Italian love affair. He could not comprehend how repulsive to a woman of refinement such stories are, and she, on her part, was properly disgusted with his coarseness. He proceeded to justify her opinion of his deterioration by taking, in practical though not formal marriage, Christiane Vulpius, a curly-haired, red-cheeked, plump young damsel, whose only merits were her health, physical beauty, and skill in housekeeping. Within less than a month he had installed this female in his house, and was living with her as his wife. Frau von Stein did not learn of the relation between the pair until the following year, and then, although Goethe blunderingly tried to convince her that it would not conflict with his devotion to her, she insisted that he must give up either Christiane or herself. He, man-like, stood by his new love, and, thereafter, for years, his intercourse with Frau von Stein was purely casual. She refused to answer his letters, and had his portrait taken down from the wall of her room. He met her at court and at friends' houses, but she treated him as a stranger.

How keenly Frau von Stein felt Goethe's defection may be imagined. It was to her a calamity worse than his death. The dead are buried out of sight, and their memory is refined and glorified by the very affection which they inspired. But the living, fallen in our esteem, and, as it were, degrading the ideal we once had of them, are a constant thorn in the flesh. What they are reminds us only too painfully of what they once were, and does not allow the wounded heart to heal. This was the effect produced upon Frau von Stein by the presence of Goethe after his return from Italy. Caroline von Beulwitz writes

CHRISTIANE VULPIUS.

of her to Schiller in 1789: "She was sunk in silent grief over her relations with Goethe, and, so, appeared to me truer and more harmonious than in unnatural indifference or contempt." In 1791 Frau von Stein herself writes to her son Fritz: "Write to Goethe; there are already letters from the living to the dead." In 1795 she says to Schiller's wife: "It seems to me as if I had for some years been shut up in a South Sea island, and had only just begun to think of the way home." In another letter to Schiller's wife in 1796 she says, referring to Herder's cynicism: "Nothing cures one of such a condition like having a really painful experience. Thus was I, by Goethe's departure, cured of all my previous sorrows. I can bear everything and forgive everything." With all this she evinced a certain degree of feminine pique. Her friend the Duchess Louise had to chide her for the bitterness with which she spoke of her old lover, and her resentment against the woman who had taken him from her knew no bounds. She called her "that creature," Goethe's "demoiselle," and as late as 1801 she wrote to her son Fritz that Goethe had passed her in the park with his "chambermaid" at his side, and that she put up her parasol to avoid saluting him. She even ridiculed Goethe's own personal appearance, saying in a letter to Fritz, in 1796, that he seemed to her to have grown "horribly fat," and, referring to his own phrase in his letter from Carlsbad of Aug. 23, 1786, before quoted, she remarks: "He has, indeed, gone back to the earth from whence we were taken." Elsewhere she calls him "poor Goethe" and "the fat privy-councillor," and says that she pities him. His literary productions she depreciates in the same way. She finds them inferior in refinement and elevation to his earlier works, remarking of "Hermann and Dorothea," which appeared in 1797: "It is a pity that the illusion of the wife who cooks at the cleanly hearth should be destroyed by Miss Vulpius." Speaking also of the second part of "Wilhelm Meister," published in 1796, she characterizes the female personages in it as "women of indecent behavior," and says that "where noble feelings in human nature are occasionally brought into action the whole is daubed with mud, in order to leave nothing heaven-like, and as if the devil wished to show that the world is not mistaken in him, and that no one should believe him to be better than he is."

But time, which deadens all passions, finally allayed much of the irritation which Frau von Stein felt towards Goethe, while his uniform good-nature and the kindness with which he cared for her son Fritz helped to soften her feelings towards him. His friendship with Schiller, whose wife was also her intimate friend, created an additional bond of union; his dangerous illness in 1801 revealed to her how dear he was still to her at the bottom of her heart, and thus, step by step, something like affection was restored between the pair. But the charm of the old days was gone, the formal "you" appears in his letters to her in place of the "thou" which marks those of the former years, and they were no longer the impetuous autographs sent two or three times a day, but were written at great intervals and by the hand of a secretary.

Frau von Stein died peacefully of old age in 1827, five years before Goethe, having left instructions that, in order to avoid giving him pain, her coffin should not be carried past his dwelling. He himself did not attend her funeral, but sent his son to represent him. Since her burial a new path has been laid out in the cemetery over her grave, and nothing now marks the spot where her remains repose.

MOZART AND ALOYSIA WEBER.

LIKE all men of artistic temperament, Mozart was extremely impressible by the charms of women. His love affairs, which commenced early, were many and frequent, but only one of them, the last before his marriage, was at all serious, or productive of any great effect upon his character. The object of his passion in this instance was Aloysia Weber, a cousin of the composer, Carl Maria von Weber, and the elder sister of the Constance Weber who afterwards became his wife.

Mozart's wonderful musical genius and the surpassing excellence of his productions have quite overshadowed, in common estimation, his personal merit. Indeed, a conviction prevails that his intellectual abilities were inferior, his character weak, and his habits dissipated. The truth, on the contrary, is that he was extremely intelligent, his weakness was nothing but the necessary accompaniment of a warm and affectionate temper, and his dissipation almost entirely imaginary. He was, indeed, fond of wine, as he was of women, but he was as far from being a drunkard as he was from being a libertine. All the evidence goes to show that his conduct was, from first to last, morally irreproachable, and that his misfortunes came from his unselfishness, and from the too great confidence which he placed in those who pretended to be his friends. As is not uncommon with men of genius, he lacked worldly wisdom, and had little of the business talent requisite for worldly success.

Mozart as a child was distinguished not more by his precocious musical talents than by his loving disposition. Andreas Schlachtner, the court trumpeter, who was an intimate friend of the Mozart family and a constant companion of the little boy, says that "Ten times a day at least he would ask me whether I loved him, and when I sometimes said, for fun, that I did not, tears sprang to his eyes, so tender and kindly was his good heart." Every night before he went to bed he would stand on a chair and sing with his father a little tune which he had himself composed to some nonsense words resembling Italian, and during the singing and after it he would kiss his father on the tip of his nose. When he was ten years old he happened to make a visit to a convent, and to find there a former friend to whom he was much attached. He immediately climbed upon him, patted his cheeks, and greeted him in a brief chant, which he afterwards wrote out into an offertory and sent to his friend as a birthday gift. For his father and mother and only sister his love knew no bounds, and he used as a child to say that when his father grew to be old he would put him in a glass case to keep him safe and have him always with him. His generosity made him a constant victim of those with whom he had dealings. He gave away some of his finest compositions, was defrauded of his copyright on many others, and he did an endless amount of work for which he received no compensation.

This natural lovingness and confidingness were encouraged rather than repressed by his education. His father, though stern, was most affectionate, and his mother was as devoted to him as he was to her. Both parents were pious Roman Catholics, and brought up their son in the strictest religious and moral principles. The father's letters to him, long after he was grown up, contain frequent injunctions to observe his devotional duties, and his answers show that these injunctions were heeded. His filial respect and obedience were as remarkable as his filial affection. His favorite saying was, "Next to God, papa," and, as we shall see, he never let his own inclinations stand in the way of the parental commands. Of his principles in regard to women, he says himself, writing to his father at the age of twenty-two: "Believe what you please of me, only nothing bad. There are people who think no one

ROMANTIC IDEAS.

can love a poor girl without evil designs. But I am no Brunetti, no Misliweczeck. I am a Mozart, and though young, still a high-principled Mozart." His lofty and romantic ideas of marriage are likewise charmingly exhibited in another letter to his father, in which he says:

"Mr. von Scheidenhofen might have let me know, through you, that his wedding was soon to take place, and I would have composed a new minuet for the occasion. I cordially wish him joy; but his is, after all, only one of those money matches, and nothing else! I hope never to marry in this way. I wish to make my wife happy, but not to become rich by her means; so I will let things alone, and enjoy my golden freedom till I am so well off that I can support both wife and children. Mr. von Scheidenhofen was forced to marry a rich wife: his rank imposed this on him. The nobility must never marry from liking and love, but from interest and various other considerations. It would not at all suit a grandee to love his wife after she had done her duty and brought into the world an heir to the property. But we poor humble people are privileged not only to choose a wife who loves us and whom we love, but we may, can, and do take such a one because we are neither noble nor high born nor rich, but, on the contrary, lowly, humble, and poor. We therefore need no wealthy wife, for our riches, being in our heads, die with us, and these no man can deprive us of unless he cut them off, in which case we need nothing more."

While intellectually, apart from his musical endowments, Mozart was not a great man, his letters and all the anecdotes related of him show him to have been lively, witty, and agreeable. He could read, write, and speak Italian and French as well as he could German, and on occasion could turn out rhymes with great facility. In society, he was noted for his rollicking fun and gayety, and his remarks were often irresistibly droll. These qualities, and his convivial habits, are what gave him the reputation of being dissipated, but unjustly so. He was also a good dancer, and played billiards and skittles with great zeal and skill.

Though Mozart was extremely susceptible of love for women, and his talents should have commended him to their favor, his external appearance rather interfered with his success with them. His father and mother were reputed to be the handsomest couple in Salzburg, where they lived, but they failed to transmit to him their advantages. He was, indeed, slim and well proportioned, but his stature was small and his figure insignificant. His complexion was pale, and his face in no respect striking, except when it was illuminated by the fire of his genius in playing or in composing. His eyes were well formed and of a good size, with fine eyebrows and lashes, but as a rule they looked languid, and his gaze was restless and absent. Like all little men, he was very particular about his dress, and wore a great deal of embroidery and jewelry.

Until he was twenty-one Mozart seems never to have been allowed to go out into the world alone. In all his professional travels he was accompanied by his father, who did not leave him for a moment. At last, in September, 1777, the anxious parent reluctantly consented to remain in Salzburg, while his son went with his mother on a tour to Munich and other cities, with the purpose of ultimately visiting Paris. He bore up bravely till the travellers actually started, and then went to his bedroom exhausted with the anguish of parting. Suddenly he remembered that in his distress he had forgotten to give his son his blessing. He rushed to the window with outstretched hand, but the carriage was already out of sight.

How Mozart enjoyed his newly acquired liberty, and the use he made of it, especially with reference to the fair sex, are summed up by his father in a letter which he wrote to him at Mannheim in February, 1778. The details given in this letter present an accurate picture of Mozart's character as it appeared to one who knew him best.

"Your journey led you to Munich; you know the purpose; it was not to be accomplished. Well-meaning friends wished to have you there; you wanted to stay there. You fell into the notion of bringing a company together. I cannot repeat the particulars. At that moment you thought the project feasible. I did not; read over what I said in answer to you. You are a man of honor; would it have done you honor to depend upon ten persons and their monthly charity? Then, you were wonderfully captivated by a little singer of the theatre, and wanted nothing better than to help the German stage. Then, you explained that you could never write a comic opera! No sooner were you outside of the gate of Munich than your whole friendly company of subscribers forgot you, and what would have happened in Munich now?

"In the end God's providence showed itself. In Augsburg you had another little scene—a merry time with my brother's daughter, who must needs send you her portrait. The rest I wrote you in my first letter to Mannheim. In Wallerstein you cracked a thousand jokes, danced here and there, so that people thought you a jolly, merry, foolish, occasionally absent-minded creature, which gave Mr. Beecke the opportunity of depreciating your merit, which by your compositions and by the playing of your sister had been set in another light with the two gentlemen, for she always said: 'I am only my brother's pupil,' so that they had the greatest respect for your skill, and preferred it to the bad work of Beecke.

"In Mannheim you did nicely, to ingratiate yourself with Mr. Cannabich! It would have been fruitless if he had not sought a twofold end. The rest I have already written to you. The daughter of Mr. Cannabich was overwhelmed with praises, the picture of her temperament expressed in the adagio of the sonata; in short, she was now the favorite person. Then you made the acquaintance of Mr. Wendling. He, now, was the noblest friend, and what happened I need not repeat. In a moment comes the acquaintance with Mr. Weber. Everything else passes away; this family is now the honestest, Christianest family, and the daughter is the chief person of the tragedy to be enacted between her family and yours, and all that you, in the giddiness in which your good heart, open to everybody, has put you, imagine her without sufficient consideration to be."

Mozart had been at Mannheim since the end of October, 1777. The city was the capital of the Palatinate, the elector of which, Charles Theodore, was a noted patron of both music and literature, and had gathered at his court, besides writers like Lessing, Wieland, and Klopstock, some of the finest musicians and composers in Germany. Among them were Schweitzer, who set to music Wieland's "Alceste;" the pianist Vogler, the celebrated tenor Raaff, for whom Mozart wrote some beautiful airs; the singers Dorothea Wendling and Francisca Danzi, the violinists Cannabich and Cramer, the flutist Wendling, the oboists Le Brun and Raum, the bassoonist Ritter, and the horn-player Lang. Mozart, indeed, complains in one of his letters that the elector's orchestra surpassed his singers so much that he had to write his music more for the instruments than for the voices. That he enjoyed staying in the place immensely appears not only from his father's account just quoted, but from his own. The

Cannabich of whom his father speaks was the leader of the orchestra as well as a violinist, and to his daughter Mozart gave lessons on the piano, besides writing for her a sonata. He next met Wendling, the flute-player, who also had a daughter, Rosa, who played the piano, and for her, too, he composed a sonata.

Finally, about the beginning of the year 1778 Mozart was introduced to the Weber family and became captivated with the singing of the second daughter, Aloysia, a girl of only fifteen, who inspired him, first by her musical talent, and afterwards by her personal charms, with profound affection. His biographer, Jahn, calls it "a passionate love," and Nohl, "his first true love." The beginning of their acquaintance and of his attachment to her, Mozart describes in a letter dated Jan. 17, 1778:

"Next Wednesday I am going for some days to Kirchheim-Poland, the residence of the Princess of Orange. I have heard so much praise of her here that at last I have resolved to go. A Dutch officer, a particular friend of mine, was much upbraided for not bringing me with him when he went to offer his

New-Year's congratulations. I expect to receive at least eight louis d'or, for as she has a passionate admiration of singing, I have had four airs copied out for her. I will also present her with a symphony, for she has a very nice orchestra and gives a concert every day.

"Besides, the copying of the airs will not cost me much, for a certain Mr. Weber, who is going there with me, has copied them. He has a daughter who sings admirably and has a lovely pure voice. She is only fifteen. She fails in nothing but stage action; were it not for that she might be the prima-donna of any theatre. Her father is a downright honest German, who brings up his children well, for which very reason the girl is presented here. He has six children, five girls and a son. He and his wife and children have been obliged to live for the last fourteen years on an income of 200 florins, but, as he has always done his duty well, and has lately provided a very accomplished lady singer for the elector, he has now, actually, 400 florins. My aria for De Amicis she sings to perfection, with all its tremendous passages. She is to sing it in Kirchheim-Poland."

The visit to Kirchheim was made as intended, and by Feb. 2, 1778, Mozart was writing to his father from Mannheim an account of it. The party left Mannheim, he says, on a Friday morning in a covered carriage, and reached Kirchheim at four in the afternoon. On Saturday evening Miss Weber sang at court, and again on Tuesday and Wednesday, besides playing the piano twice. Of her performance on this instrument Mozart speaks in high praise, and adds: "What surprises me most is that she reads music so well. Only think of her playing my difficult sonatas at sight, slowly, but without missing a single note. I give you my honor I would rather hear my sonatas played by her than by Vogler." For his services and for the four symphonies which he presented to the princess he received seven louis d'or, and Aloysia, for her singing, five, which disappointed him, as he had expected that each of them would get eight louis d'or. With characteristic cheerfulness he adds: "We were not, however, losers, for I have a profit of forty-two florins, and the inexpressible pleasure of becoming better acquainted with worthy, upright Christian people and good Catholics. I regret much not having known them long ago."

What attractions Aloysia possessed beyond her musical gifts is unknown. She never became celebrated for her beauty, and her character, at her age, must have been still undeveloped. Mozart himself, writing of her three years after, says she was ungrateful to her parents and left them without assistance when she was making money for herself as a singer, and a little later, when he had fallen in love with her sister, he speaks of her as "false, unprincipled, and a coquette." But of her excellent singing and playing there was no question, and in listening to her, teaching her, and composing for her Mozart was enraptured.

One consequence of this attachment was to put an end to a project which Mozart had formed, with the approval of his mother, of proceeding to Paris in company with the flute-player, Wendling, and his daughter Rosa, Ramm, the oboist, and Ritter, the bassoonist. Wendling was to direct the party, as he professed to have a thorough knowledge of Paris and its ways. How completely Mozart's opinion of him had changed will appear from what he writes soon after the trip to Kirchheim:

"Now comes something urgent, about which I request an answer. Mamma and I have discussed the matter, and we agree that we do not like the sort of life the Wendlings lead. Wendling is a very honorable and kind man, but, unhappily, devoid of religion, and the whole family are the same. I say enough when I tell you his daughter was a most disreputable character. Ramm is a good fellow, but a libertine. I know myself, and I have such a sense of religion that I shall never do anything which I would not do before the whole world; but I am alarmed even at the very thought of being in the society of people whose mode of thinking is so entirely different from mine (and from that of all good people). But, of course, they must do as they please. I have no heart to travel with them, nor could I enjoy one pleasant hour, nor know what to talk about, for, in short, I have no great confidence in them. Friends who have no religion cannot be long our friends. I have already given them a hint of this by saying that during my absence three letters had arrived, of which I could divulge nothing further than that it was unlikely I should be able to go with them to Paris, but that perhaps I might come later, or possibly go elsewhere; so they must not depend on me. I shall be able to finish my music now quite at my ease for De Jean, who is to give me 200 florins for it.

"I can remain here as long as I please, and neither board nor lodging costs me anything. In the meantime Mr. Weber will endeavor to make various engagements for concerts with me, and then we shall travel together. If I am with him it is just as if I were with you. This is the reason that I like him so much; except in personal appearance he resembles you in all respects, and has exactly your character and mode of thinking. If my mother were not, as you know, too comfortably lazy to write, she would say precisely what I do. I must confess that I much enjoyed my excursion with them. We were pleased and merry. I heard a man converse just like you. I had no occasion to trouble myself about anything; what was torn I found repaired. In short, I was treated like a prince.

"I am so attached to this oppressed family that my greatest wish is to make them happy, and perhaps I may be able to do so. My advice is that they should go to Italy, so I am all anxiety for you to write to our good friend Lugiati, and the sooner the better, to inquire what are the highest terms given to a prima-donna in Verona; the more the better, for it is always easy to accept lower terms. Perhaps it would be possible to obtain the Ascensa in Venice. I will be answerable with my life for her singing and her doing credit to my recommendation. She has even during this short period derived much profit from me, and how much further progress she will have made by that time! I have no fears, either, with regard to her acting.

"If this plan be realized, Mr. Weber, his two daughters, and I will have the happiness of visiting my dear papa and sister for a fortnight on our way through Salzburg. My sister will find a friend and companion in Miss Weber, for, like my sister in Salzburg, she enjoys the best reputation here, owing to the careful way in which she has been brought up; the father resembles you, and the whole family that of Mozart. They have, indeed, detractors, as with us, but when it comes to the point they must confess the truth, and truth lasts longest. I should be glad to go with them to Salzburg, that you might hear her. My air that De Amicis used to sing, and the bravura air *Parto m'affretto*, and *Dalla sponda tenebrosa*, she sings splendidly. Pray do all you can to insure our going to Italy together. You know my greatest desire is to write operas.

"I will gladly write an opera for Verona for thirty zecchini, solely that Miss Weber may acquire fame by it; for if I do not I fear she may be sacrificed. Before then I hope to make so much money by visiting different places that I shall be no loser. I think we shall go to Switzerland, perhaps also to Holland: pray write me soon about this. Should we stay long anywhere the eldest daughter would be of the greatest use to us; for we could have our own *ménage*, as she understands cooking.

"Send me an answer soon, I beg. Don't forget my wish to write an opera. I could almost weep from vexation when I hear or see an aria. But Italian, not German—*seria*, not *buffa!* I have not written you all that is in my heart. My mother is satisfied with my plan."

Mozart was mistaken about his mother's approval, for she adds to his letter this postscript:

"No doubt you perceive by the accompanying letter that when Wolfgang makes new friends he would give his life for them. It is true that she does sing incomparably; still we ought not to lose sight of our own interests. I never liked his being in the society of Wendling and Ramm, but I did not venture to object to it, nor would he have listened to me, but no sooner did he know these Webers than he instantly changed his mind. In short, he prefers other people to me, for I remonstrate with him sometimes, and that he does not like. I write this quite secretly, while he is at dinner, for I don't wish him to know it."

The project which Mozart had formed of giving up his proposed visit to Paris and of attempting instead to establish his beloved as a prima-donna in an Italian town seemed to his father sheer lunacy. He took time to prepare himself, and in two long letters, one dated Feb. 12 and the other Feb. 16, he went over the ground carefully, and exhausted every argument of prudence, reason, and affection to defeat the scheme. He recounted his own privations, the personal sacrifices he had made to educate his son, and the dependence of the entire family upon his success in his career. "The future destiny of your old parents and of your loving sister is in your hands." "I place in your filial love all my confidence and all my hope." "It depends on your decision whether you shall be a common musician whom the world forgets, or a renowned composer of whom posterity and history shall speak; whether, infatuated with a pretty face, you one day breathe your last upon straw, your wife and children starving, or whether, after a happy, Christianly spent life, you die in honor and wealth, respected, as well as your family, by the whole world." And he ends with this touching appeal:

"I know that you love me not alone as your father, but as your truest and surest friend; that you know and consider that our fortune and misfortune, yes, my longer life or early death, are, so to speak, under God, in your hands. If I know you, I have nothing but happiness to expect, which in your absence, which robs me of the fatherly pleasure of seeing you and embracing you, is my only comfort.

Live as a good Catholic Christian, love and fear God, pray to Him with devotion and faith and full earnestness, and conduct yourself in so Christian a manner that if I never see you again my deathbed may not be sorrowful. I give you from my heart my fatherly blessing, and I am till death your faithful father and surest friend."

The result to which all these affectionate exhortations were directed was to induce Mozart to quit Mannheim at once and start for Paris. "Off with you to Paris, and that soon; put yourself into the company of great people. *Aut Cæsar, aut nihil!* The single thought of seeing Paris ought to have preserved you from passing fancies. From Paris proceeds fame and name for a man of great talent, over the whole world. The nobility treat genius with the greatest condescension, esteem, and courtesy."

The appeal was successful. Mozart replied on the 19th of February, submissively:

"I always thought that you would disapprove of my journey with the Webers, but I never had any such intentions—I mean, under present circumstances. I gave them my word of honor to write to you to that effect. Mr. Weber does not know how we stand,

and I certainly shall tell it to no one. I wish my position had been such that I had no cause to consider any one else, and that we were all independent; but in the intoxication of the moment I forgot the present impossibility of the affair, and also to tell you what I had done. The reasons of my not being now in Paris must be evident to you from my last two letters. If my mother had not first begun on this subject I certainly should have gone with my friends; but when I saw that she did not like it I began to dislike it also. When people lose confidence in me I am apt to lose confidence in myself. The days when, standing on a chair, I sang *Oragna fiagata fa*, and kissed the tip of your nose, are indeed gone by; but still, have my reverence, love, and obedience towards yourself ever failed on that account? I say no more."

The surrender cost Mozart an illness which for two days confined him to the house, and on the 22d of February he writes: "You must forgive my not writing much at this time. But I really cannot. I am so afraid of bringing back my headache, and besides I feel no inclination to write to-day. It is impossible to write all we think, at least I find it to be so. I would rather say it than write it. My last letter told you the whole thing just as it stands." The next week he devoted to composing an aria suited to Aloysia's voice, and gave it to her as a farewell present. On the 7th of March he writes to his father again:

"I have received your letter of the 26th February, and am much obliged to you for all the trouble you have taken about the arias, which are quite accurate in every respect. 'Next to God, papa,' was my motto when a child, and I still think the same. You are right when you say that 'knowledge is power;' besides, except your trouble and fatigue, you will have no cause for regret, and Miss Weber certainly deserves your kindness. I only wish that you could hear her sing my new aria, which I lately mentioned to you. I say hear *her* sing it, because it seems made expressly for her; a man like you, who really understands what *portamento* in singing means, would certainly feel the most intense pleasure in hearing her."

Having taken his resolution, Mozart lost no time in executing it. He went around and bade adieu to his friends, ending with the Webers. He describes his parting visit to them in the first letter which he wrote to his father from Paris. After recounting how Mrs. Weber knitted two pairs of mittens for him, and how Mr. Weber gave him a copy of Molière's plays, saying to his mother that he was the family's benefactor and best friend, he concludes:

"The day before I set off they would insist on my supping with them, but I managed to give them two hours before supper instead. They never ceased thanking me and saying they only wished they were in a position to testify their gratitude, and when I went away they all wept. Pray forgive me, but really tears come to my eyes when I think of it. Weber came down-stairs with me, and remained standing at the door till I turned the corner and called out 'Adieu.'"

Mozart arrived in Paris with his mother March 13, 1778, and immediately set about visiting great people, giving concerts, and writing music. He gained reputation by his efforts, but not much money, and had besides to suffer the affliction of losing his mother by death, about the end of July. At last, weary, sad, and hopeless of success, he gave up, at the beginning of October, and turned his face homeward. During his stay in Paris he had but little correspondence with Miss Weber, though he frequently mentions her in his letters to his father, and expresses his satisfaction with her success in her profession. The elector of the Palatinate had early in the year become elector of Bavaria, and had removed his court from Mannheim to Munich, which, naturally, compelled the removal with him of all the artists dependent upon his patronage, the Webers among them. This was the cause of the final catastrophe. Mozart's beloved had obtained the appointment of court singer at Munich, with a liberal salary, and in her new surroundings had ceased to love the man whose departure she had wept over a few months before. He arrived at Munich on the 25th of December, full of eagerness to see her, and hastened to call upon her. She received him like a stranger, and the story goes that, immediately on perceiving the alteration in her sentiments, he sat down at a piano in the room and sang aloud the song, "I gladly leave the maid who will have none of me." But that her inconstancy deeply affected him appears from the letter he wrote to his father a day or two afterwards:

"I write from the house of Mr. Becke. I arrived here safely, God be praised, on the 25th, but I have been unable to write to you till now. I reserve everything till our glad, joyous meeting, when I can once more have the happiness of conversing with you, for to-day I can only weep. I have far too sensitive a heart. In the meantime I must tell you that the day before I left Kaisersheim I received the sonatas; so I shall be able to present them myself to the electoress. I only delay leaving here till the opera is given, when I intend immediately to leave Munich, unless I were to find it would be very beneficial and useful to remain here for some time longer. In this case, I feel convinced, quite convinced, that you would not only be satisfied I should do so, but would yourself advise it.

"I naturally write very badly, for I never learned to write; still, in my whole life I never wrote worse than this very day, for I am really unfit for anything; my heart is too full of tears. I hope you will soon write to me and comfort me. Address me *poste restante* and then I can fetch the letter myself. I am staying with the Webers. I think, after all, it would be better, far better, to enclose your letter to our friend, Becke.

"I intend (I mention it to you in the strictest secrecy) to write a mass here. All my best friends advise my doing so. I cannot tell you what friends Cannabich and Raaff have been to me. Now farewell, my kindest and most beloved father! Write to me soon.

"A happy new year! More I cannot bring myself to write to-day."

Aloysia's conduct was not unnatural nor inexplicable. She was but fifteen years old, and, most probably, never had any deeper feeling for Mozart than admiration of his talents and gratitude for his devotion to her. Had he remained constantly in company with her he might have retained his place in her heart, but "out of sight out of mind." A girl of fifteen easily forgets and quickly changes. Consequently, when Aloysia Weber saw Mozart in December, he was to her quite another being than the Mozart whom she had loved, after a childish fashion, in March. Years afterwards she confessed that when he came to her at Munich all she saw in him was that he was a little man, and from other sources we learn that she was displeased at his coat, which, as he was in mourning for his mother, was, after the Paris fashion, black, with red buttons! On such trifles hang men's success

MOZART.

with women, and especially with women of Aloysia's age and character.

Mozart seems to have made no effort to recover his lost ground with Aloysia. Perhaps he, too, was less deeply interested than he thought he was, and enjoyed the restoration of his freedom more than he was pained by his beloved's faithlessness. Notwithstanding his disappointment, he continued to cherish for her the admiration of a musician, and in January, 1779, within a fortnight after the painful interview with her just mentioned, he composed for her a florid air, specially adapted to show off the capacities of her voice, which ranged from G in the treble clef to the G two octaves higher, and, as one of her critics says, was like a Cremona violin. The accompaniment was also written for oboe and bassoon, *obligati*, to be played by his friends Ramm and Ritter. The text was from Gluck's "Alceste," and commences with the words "*Popoli di Tessaglia.*" That he did not for a long time cease to love her appears from a passage in one of his letters from Vienna, written in May, 1781, after her marriage with the actor Lange: "With the Lange I was a fool, it is true; what is a man not when he is in love? Yet I loved her really, and I feel that she is not yet without interest to me, which is lucky for me, because her husband is a jealous fool, and allows her no freedom, and I am, therefore, seldom able to see her." He had the satisfaction to find, as time went on, that his opinion of her musical ability had been sound, and not biassed by a lover's partiality, and he continued to write music for her, and to take pleasure in her triumphs. From Munich she went to Vienna, became there a prima-donna of the foremost rank, and married, as has been said, an actor. She did not live happily with her husband, and Nohl, one of Mozart's biographers, speaks of her career as follows:

"Neither happiness nor riches brightened Aloysia's life, nor the peace of mind arising from the consciousness of purity of heart. Not till she was an aged woman, and Mozart long dead, did she recognize what he really had been. She liked to talk about him and his friendship, and in thus recalling the brightest memories of her youth, some of that lovable charm that Mozart had imparted to her, as he did to all with whom he had intercourse, seemed to revive. Every one was captivated by her gay, unassuming manner, her freedom from all the usual *virtuoso* caprices in society, and her readiness to give pleasure by her talent to every one who had any knowledge or love of music. It seems as if a portion of the tender spirit with which Mozart once loved her had passed into her soul and brought forth fresh leaves from a withered stem."

Further evidence of Aloysia's tardy regret for her youthful lover is found in some words in Italian which she wrote at the end of an autograph copy of an air composed by him for her in Vienna in 1788. "In thy happy days think sometimes of '*Popoli di Tessaglia*,'" referring to the composition at Munich in 1779. She died in 1827.

After a year spent with his father in Salzburg, Mozart went back to Munich, and thence to Vienna, to join his patron, the Archbishop of Salzburg, who was in attendance at the imperial court. Here he continued his intimacy with the Webers, and, by a not uncommon metamorphosis of sentiment, transferred to Constance Weber the love which he had formerly felt for her sister. After much opposition, both from his father and her mother, and the usual lovers' quarrels, the couple were married in August, 1782. Mozart died nine years later, in November, 1791, at a little less than thirty-six years of age. His trials and troubles, his artistic achievements, and the vicissitudes of his fortune hold a prominent place in the records of the lives of men of genius. His wife seems to have been more of a burden than a help to him, yet he loved her tenderly, and his letters to her are characterized by the sweetest and most affectionate spirit. For his old love, her sister, he retained friendship to the last.

CAVOUR.

CAVOUR AND THE UNKNOWN.

AMONG the private papers of the celebrated Italian statesman, Count Camillo di Cavour, were found, after his death in 1861, a series of letters from a lady, whose name has never been divulged to the public, written at various dates from 1830 to 1839, and filed away by him as if for permanent preservation. In a diary he had kept from 1833 to 1835, were also found a number of entries referring to the writer of the letters in question. These documents, with many others, were intrusted by his niece and representative, the Marchesa Giuseppina di Cavour, to Domenico Berti, the historian, for the preparation of a biography of her uncle during his early years, which was published at Rome in 1866, under the title of "Il Conte di Cavour avanti il 1848." One chapter of this work is devoted to the narrative of Cavour's connection with the lady whose letters he had so carefully preserved, giving extracts from them, and passages from his diary explaining them.

The first of the letters is dated about the middle of the year 1830. Cavour was then an officer of engineers, barely twenty years of age, and was stationed at Genoa. His acquaintance with the writer of the letters apparently began at Turin the previous winter. The lady was presumably nearly of Cavour's own age, but who she was, except that she was of noble family, we are not told. Cavour calls her "L'Inconnue" (the Unknown), and Berti adopts the appellation. Whether, when Cavour first knew her she was married or single, also does not appear, but Berti, referring to events which took place in 1835, speaks of her as then having a husband. He begins his narrative abruptly :

"Camillo Cavour had not yet surrendered his commission when he met a lady who was to make a profound and permanent impression upon his heart.

"Sympathy and affection sprang up between the two simultaneously. He loved in her the grace, the charms of her person; the sweetness, the elevation of her soul; the cultivation and the keenness of her intellect. She loved in him his noble, generous, honest nature, the vivacity of his person and fascinating manners, and, above all, his vigorous genius. 'I am sure,' she writes in her first letter, 'that the day will come when your genius will be appreciated. My warmest wishes are that everything may turn out as you desire.'"

Of course, the youthful Cavour of 1830 was not the Cavour whose career as a journalist, a politician, and a statesman fairly commenced only eighteen years afterwards; but he had already begun to manifest the ability which in later years made him foremost among his countrymen. That the object of his love was unusually intelligent, as well as personally attractive, is plain both from the portions of her letters which Berti copies and from what is said of her in an obituary notice which he appends to his narrative. She cultivated her mind assiduously, could read, write, and speak English, German, Italian, and French, though, like Cavour, who, born and educated in Savoy, did not master Italian until he was thirty, she usually employed French in conversation and in her correspondence. She wrote much which was never published, among other things an essay on Shakespeare's "Romeo and Juliet," which she sent to Cavour, and which, as Berti tells us, he set above Rousseau's "Julie." In politics she took a lively interest, and was a more ardent republican than Cavour, who, however, eventually converted her to his less extreme views. Her temperament, naturally melancholy, was rendered still more so by ill-health, and, apparently, by unhappy family relations. As we shall see, she was capable of the most passionate and romantic love, and she carried her devotion to Cavour to a pitch that made her family at one time think her reason was affected.

Whatever led to the first meeting of the lovers, they soon separated, and Berti tells us that among the lady's letters to Cavour are found only one dated in 1830, one in 1831, two in 1832, one in 1833, and nothing in 1834 before June. Cavour takes upon himself the blame for this estrangement.

"I preserved a tender and painful remembrance of her; I found myself often regretting that my own stupidity, coupled with unfortunate circumstances, had prevented my forming with this sweet and lovable woman a connection which would have thrown such a charm over my sad and monotonous existence; but, to tell the truth, there remained in my heart for her no sentiment of love nor of passion. All my desire was limited to seeing her again, to being useful to her, and to vowing to her a sincere and disinterested friendship." Whether this means he might have married her but did not, or whether what he regretted was something less honorable, is not plain. Anyway, towards the end of June, 1834, when he was at Grinzane, a town half a day's journey distant from Turin, he received from her a little note saying she was at Turin, and wanted to see him. He had not heard from her since January, 1833, when she answered a letter which he had written her "to express to her," he says in his diary, "the sympathy which her long misfortunes had excited in me." He knew only that she had been living at Milan in a continual state of suffering and sickness. His diary continues:

"I cannot describe the sentiments which at this moment agitated my heart. Uncertainty as to the motives which led the Unknown to the step troubled me cruelly. Was it a simple desire to explain her past conduct, and to establish with me amicable relations in conformity with the sentiments she had expressed to me in her last letter? Or, had she suddenly succumbed to the passion against which she had vainly so long struggled? I fancied I could detect in the few phrases of which her short note was composed, desires, and an ill-repressed tenderness, but this must have been only an illusion of my vanity, for there was not one word which indicated a change in my favor. I could not contain myself. Tormented by the fear of finding her no longer in Turin, by uncertainty as to the reception she had arranged for me, and by an irresistible desire to express to her all the gratitude, affection, and devotion with which her behavior to me had inspired me, I resolved to set out instantly. Abandoning fifty matters of business which remained for me to finish, and braving the insupportable heat of the sun, I started at one o'clock. Changing horses at Bra, without stopping, I arrived at Turin at eight. I ran home, changed my dress, and, without losing a moment, flew to the hotel where the Unknown was staying. I was told that she had just gone to the opera. Without delay I ran thither, plunged into the pit, ran my eye over the boxes, and in the sixth from the left on the first tier I perceived a lady in deep mourning, and wearing on the sweetest of countenances the traces of long and cruel suffering. It was she. She recognized me at once; she had followed me with her eyes until I left the pit to come to her. God! what charm in her look; how much tenderness and love! Whatever I may do for her in future, I can never repay her the happiness she made me feel in that moment. Her box was full, and insupportable bores overwhelmed my poor friend with the most vapid and insipid talk. Vainly did our eyes endeavor to express the sentiments of our hearts. We burned with impatience. At last we were left alone a moment, but the abundance of the things we had to say choked the words in our throats. After a long silence she said to me: 'What have you thought of me?' 'Can you ask me?' I answered. 'You have suffered a great deal.' 'Have I suffered? Oh, yes! I have suffered much.' These are all the words I remember." . . .

Cavour goes on to say that he quitted the Unknown that evening full of hope, love, regret, and remorse. He believed in the sincerity of her passion, he was proud to intoxication of a love so pure, so constant, and so disinterested, but, on the other hand, when he thought of his conduct towards her, and represented to himself the terrible sufferings which she had endured because of him, and of which he had always before his eyes the traces upon her beautiful and sad countenance, he was enraged with himself and accused himself of insensibility, of cruelty, of infamy.

On returning home he learned that his father, supposing him still to be at Grinzane, was coming to see him the next day. In order to prevent this useless journey he started off at midnight on foot, being unable to procure a conveyance, and arrived at his father's house at three o'clock in the morning. With the expansiveness of the Latin races—it is said that a Frenchman, if he cannot find any other confidant, will tell of his *bonnes fortunes* to his mother, and we shall see, later on, that Cavour actually did this, and even confided in his brother—he related to his father the whole story and obtained from him permission to return to Turin. At half-past eight in the evening that same day he called on the Unknown at her hotel in Turin and had the good fortune to find her alone. Her depressed air and sombre attire produced on him the most painful impression. She was the image of suffering, and who had caused that suffering? Explanations were made on both sides, and, finally, emboldened by the sweetness of her looks, Cavour took her hand and pressed it to his lips. "Do you forgive me?" he said. She could resist no longer. She bent her brow to his, and her lips sought his in a kiss of love and of peace. Then she told him the whole story of her sad life, in doing which she endeavored by all means, he says, to avoid reproaching him, but vividly portraying the violence of her passion for him.

Cavour was transported. He writes in his diary: "Unhappy man! I am unworthy of so much love! How, how shall I recompense it? Ah! I swear never, never to forget, never to abandon this celestial woman. My existence shall be consecrated to her. She shall be the purpose of my life, the sole object of my care, of my efforts. May the curse of Heaven smite my head if I ever wilfully cause her the least pain or offend the least sentiment of this perfect and adorable heart." And for a few months he makes only occasional references to the political matters which had previously engrossed his mind. Once he says: "Lord Grey and his whole Ministry have resigned without my paying attention to it. It is astounding. I recognize myself no longer."

Four days after this interview the Unknown left Turin for a bathing resort, but she had hardly departed before Cavour wrote her a fiery letter, expressing at length his passion for her. Not getting an answer so soon as he expected, he wrote in the same strain a second letter, more passionate than the first, begging her to break up her existing relations and fly with him to another country. Upon reflection, however, he saw the madness of this proposition, and confessed that he had done wrong to ask the woman he loved to violate her duty. Then came the answer to his first letter, and the sweetness and tenderness of its tone confirmed him in his good resolutions. "My God," he writes in his diary, "turn away from this angel of grace and affection the cup of bitterness and I will drink it to the dregs!" Still he could not refrain from joining her, and remaining in her company three days, when she went back to Turin.

The pair had hardly separated before the Unknown wrote to her lover a letter, in the course of which she says:

"I do not know why happiness leaves in me more profound traces than unhappiness. These three days, I assure you, have effaced the remembrance of many cruel years. I preserve them in my memory as an inexhaustible treasure of consolation for the days of sadness which await me. I shall reflect, then, that time passes, but that love abides forever. We know it will, we who, not content to live here for fleeting years, dare look forward to an endless future of love and of happiness. I have told you, Camillo, my soul is only a reflection of thine; without thee I am nothing; let the light be intercepted, and I shall cease to exist. I shall follow thee everywhere; let no one hope to separate me from thee. Relatives, friends, I renounce all rather than cease to see thee and to write to thee. I shall perhaps encounter opposition. I foresee it without alarm. I feel my strength. I feel that nothing can subdue me so long as I am as sure as I am of thy love. Thy heart answers to mine, and between us it is, as thy motto says : 'For life or for death.' If I deceive myself may I fall to dust before being undeceived!"

She continues in this strain at length, and two hours later she adds a postscript, telling of an encounter in regard to him she had with her mother in the presence of her family. Her mother had reproached her for her conduct, saying that it was useless for her to love when her life was so soon to end; to which she had answered that for that very reason she ought to satiate herself with love.

Shortly after these events the Unknown quitted Turin, taking with her Cavour's letters, which she read over and over in her carriage, writing to him whenever she halted. This epistolary outpour she kept up after her arrival home, writing sometimes thrice a day. She had nothing new to say, but repeated the same sentiments of love in various forms.

As Cavour had confided to his father the renewal of his intimacy with the Unknown, so, as his passion swelled in volume and intensity, his breast was unable to contain it and it overflowed upon his mother. He went to see her, opened his whole heart to her, and gave her the letters of his beloved to read. His mother, Berti tells us, was moved to tears by them, and when Cavour communicated this manifestation of maternal sympathy to the Unknown, she responded with an equal gush of affection: "Oh, Camillo," she writes, "why cannot I throw myself at thy mother's feet, and express to her all the gratitude, respect, and love which are inspired by the tender interest she takes in me!" And she adds that she sees in the mother's approval an excuse for a passion regarded by the world as a fault.

A long letter from the Unknown is devoted to the subject of religion. She had early discovered the emptiness of mere religious formalities, but, as she says, without losing her religious sentiments, her admiration of the Scriptures—particularly the Psalms and the Gospels—and her belief in a life after death, " I perceived the absurdity of the practices of Catholicism, and by the greatest good fortune did not cease to believe, so that my heart was not depressed. Since then my religion has made me regard death not only with joy as the end of my sufferings, but also as the commencement of an existence which shall fulfil my desire at once of loving and of knowing."

In another letter she discusses the future of the Roman Catholic Church, concluding that it must become more free and liberal if it would continue to exist.

As has been said before, the Unknown was in politics more radical than Cavour. She deified Armand Carrel and regarded Raspail and Trelat as heroes, admired Mazzini, and contributed money to the support of the revolutionary journal, the *Giovane Italia.* Cavour was willing that she should worship Armand Carrel, but he ridiculed all her other idols until she gave them up, saying, "Thou hast only to tell me what to will and to think, and I will will and think it."

Though Cavour had not at this time entered upon his active political career, he was fitting himself for it by a careful study of the history of Europe, of the institutions and government of other countries, and of social and educational science. The fruits of his labors he occasionally embodied in writing and submitted to his beloved. On her part, she eagerly aided him by her counsel and her criticisms, and she jealously insisted that she should be the first to read his productions, reproaching him bitterly on one occasion for publishing an essay without first showing it to her. Everything goes to prove that after the outburst of passion which followed their meeting at the opera in Turin, her relations with Cavour were purely sentimental and intellectual. Her beauty, according to all that we are told, was not of the kind which creates a desire for actual possession; and even if it had been, she was separated from her lover too effectually by distance and by the barriers interposed by her family for it to exercise its power. Her love was purely the desire of loving, coupled with admiration for her lover's talents. She writes to him "To find a being who should accept the wreck of my existence, partake my sorrows, love me, in a word, was a happiness I had no right to expect. Fate has marked thee for my last support — thee, full of strength, life, talent — thee, destined perhaps to run the most brilliant career, to contribute to the welfare of the world. I am thine — dost thou comprehend it? — thine, soul of my life! It is my happiness, it is all that I could dream of as the most beautiful, the most brilliant. In return, O Camillo, I ask nothing of thee! Follow only the dictates of thy heart. May they lead thee to thy constant friend!" And to the very end she protested that she desired no more of him than this. His feelings seem to have been those of pity and tenderness — not, perhaps, without some alloy of gratified vanity — rather than those of vigorous manly affection.

That such was the case is proved by the fact that at the end of six months passed in this delightful epistolary intercourse, he grew tired of it. His letters began to be less frequent, and, finally, in the course of 1835, they ceased altogether. Engrossed with his work, his studies, and the care of his father's landed estates, he seems almost entirely to have forgotten the woman to whom he had, only the year before, vowed to consecrate his life. On her part, though she continued to cherish for him ardent attachment, she meekly accepted her fate. As Berti says, "Her very supreme sweetness was more fitted to inspire respect and friendship than to bind a man strongly to her." The case was only one among many exemplifications of the familiar lines in "Don Juan:"

> "Man's love is of man's life a thing apart;
> 'Tis woman's whole existence."

When, after a while, her friends urged upon the Unknown a reconciliation with her family, Cavour sided with them, and she obeyed him. For the next few years nothing more is recorded of her. She retired from the world and lived in seclusion, with only two lady friends for companions. Cavour set out upon a tour through France and England, and Berti hints that other objects received from him the adoration he once so passionately bestowed upon the

Unknown, and that she knew it. But she only buried her love more deeply in the recesses of her heart, and kept it there.

At last, early in 1839, a slanderous attack upon Cavour called forth a letter of sympathy to him from the Unknown, to which he must have replied, because she writes to him on the 3d of March as follows, using the formal "you" instead of the affectionate "thou" of her earlier epistles:

"I have not spoken of you for many years, and this silence would perhaps have been prolonged to the end of my life if a horrible letter which reached me on Monday had not overthrown my most determined resolutions. Monsieur D. has, without doubt, told you what took place.

"I thank you for the remembrance you have preserved of me. I should not answer you if I thought my duty forbade it. But time and misfortune have entirely restored to me my liberty. No bond forbids me to assure you of my friendship. This letter I might post at the street corner. As to the happiness which you counsel me to seek, it is perhaps nearer at hand than you imagine, for suffering and the very injustice I have endured have essentially destroyed my peace of mind. Agitation fatigues me, wearies me. My repose is, perhaps, sombre, but I am pleased with it, because it is permanent. Long-continued solitude has made me discover that I do not need diversion. I dare to say that I have learned to suffice to myself. I have, however, a few lady friends; one of them has had the kindness to see Monsieur D., to explain what had been written to me about you. The other, who is more particularly, more intimately, the confidant of my heart, is an angelic young person named —— ——. It is she whom I love most in the world.

"I do not ask you to write to me, but I thank you for having written. It is sweet to be assured that everything is not effaced on this earth."

It will be observed that in this letter the Unknown hints both that she was a widow and that her death was approaching. A subsequent letter, the last of the series, apparently intended to be delivered after the catastrophe, conveys the announcement in plain language, this time reverting to the tender "thou."

"The woman who loved thee is dead. She was not beautiful—she had suffered too much. What she lacked she knew better than thou. She is dead, I tell thee, and in the domain of death she has met with former rivals.

"If she has yielded to them the palm of beauty in this world, where the senses demand to be seduced, here she excels them all. None has loved thee as she did, none! for, O Camillo, thou hast never appreciated the vastness of her love. How could she have revealed it to thee? Human words could not express it; no act, however devoted it appeared to thee, was more than the shadow of what her heart desired to produce for thee. So, thou hast often seen me silent and concentrated, renouncing an incomplete manifestation, and hoping within myself that the truth would have its day. What! does this immense sentiment exist to be forever suppressed? Shall not this burning germ have its full development? Is so much love created but to consume the bosom that harbors it?

"Camillo! farewell! At the moment I write these lines I am firmly resolved never to see thee again. Thou wilt read them—I hope—but when an insurmountable barrier shall have been raised up between us, when I shall have received the great initiation into the secrets of the tomb, when perhaps—I tremble in supposing it—thou shalt have forgotten me."

How soon after this letter was written the Unknown died is not told, but it could not have been long. Cavour probably received no further communication from her, for this one he seems to have sent to his brother, or to some other intimate friend, to read, with an endorsement in his own handwriting: "If you doubt read this letter. Return it to me afterwards, for it is perhaps the last souvenir which I shall have of her whom I have caused to suffer so much, without her ever complaining of me." At all events, with it closes the story of the affair, so far as it has been published. Berti hints in a tantalizing way at a diary kept by the lady, in which she wrote down the details of her long and painful agony, but that is all. Cavour showed no further interest in her beyond filing and keeping her letters. He gradually became more and more immersed in political affairs, and, when the revolutions of 1848 broke out, he entered upon the public career which made him famous. He never married, for the reason, he says himself, that his unequal character would not permit him to make a woman happy. It is more likely that absorption in his work and advancing years rendered him less and less susceptible to woman's charms, and that he finally became proof against them. Still, once in his life, at least, he knew what it was to be the subject of the tender passion, notwithstanding that its reign in his heart was brief, and that the impression it made upon him was evanescent.

JANE WELSH CARLYLE.

IRVING AND MRS. CARLYLE.

THE story of the Rev. Edward Irving's love for Jane Baillie Welsh, afterwards the wife of Thomas Carlyle, of her love for him, and of the heroic sacrifice which both made of their happiness to a lofty and perhaps mistaken sense of duty, is one of the most pathetic ever known.

Jane Baillie Welsh was born July 14, 1801, at Haddington, a small town lying seventeen and a half miles east of Edinburgh. Her father was the leading physician of the place, a man of genial, kindly character, and of considerable intellectual force. Her mother was also possessed of a good intellect, and, as Carlyle tells us, "was unusually beautiful, but strangely sad. Eyes bright, as if with many tears behind them."

From both parents, therefore, Jane inherited talent, and from her mother beauty. Of her appearance in childhood her friend, Miss Jewsbury, says that "she was remarkable for her large black eyes, with their long, curved lashes. As a girl she was extremely pretty; a graceful and beautifully formed figure, upright and supple; a delicate complexion of creamy white, with a pale rose tint in the cheeks; lovely eyes, full of fire and softness, and with great depths of meaning. Her head was finely formed, with a noble arch and a broad forehead. Her other features were not regular, but they did not prevent her conveying all the impression of being beautiful. Her voice was clear and full of subtle intonations and capable of great variety of expression. She had it under full control." To this Mr. Froude, her friend and biographer, adds: "But beauty was only the second thought which her appearance suggested, the first was intellectual vivacity;" and speaking of her as he first saw her, when she was forty-eight, he says: "Her features were not regular, but I thought I had never seen a more interesting-looking woman. Her hair was raven black, her eyes dark, soft, sad, with dangerous light in them." Her charms, whatever they were, must have been great, to win for her as they did the title of the "Flower of Haddington," and to captivate two such men as Irving and Carlyle; and Miss Jewsbury says that "a relative of hers told me that every man who spoke to her for five minutes felt impelled to make her an offer of marriage."

Jane was an only child, and as it had been a great disappointment to her father that she was not a boy, he resolved to educate her as a boy. In this purpose his wife did not agree with him, and the pair had frequent discussions of the subject, to which the little girl listened attentively and with a better comprehension than was suspected. The result is thus told by Irving's biographer, Mrs. Oliphant·

"Her ambition was roused; to be educated like a boy became the object of her entire thought, and set her little mind working with independent projects of its own. She resolved to take the first step in this awful but fascinating course on her own responsibility. Having already divined that Latin was the first grand point of distinction, she made up her mind to settle the matter by learning Latin. A copy of the *Rudiments* was quickly found in the lumber room of the house, and a tutor not much further off in a humble student of the neighborhood. The little scholar had a dramatic instinct. She did not pour forth her first lesson as soon it was acquired, or rashly betray her secret. She waited the fitting place and moment. It was evening, when dinner had softened out the asperities of the day; the doctor sat in luxurious leisure in his dressing-gown and slippers, sipping his coffee, and all the cheerful accessories of the fireside picture were complete. The little heroine had arranged herself under the table, under the crimson folds of the cover, which concealed her small person. All was still; the moment had arrived. '*Penna, pennæ, pennam !*' burst forth the little voice in breathless steadiness. The result may be imagined; the doctor smothered his child with kisses, and even the mother herself had not a word to say; the victory was complete."

Another account of the same incident, substantially agreeing with Mrs. Oliphant's, was given to Carlyle, shortly after his wife's death, by Miss Jewsbury, as she heard it from Mrs. Carlyle herself. Miss Jewsbury's version contains the further detail that, after reciting her noun, the little girl went up to her father and said: "I want to learn Latin; please let me be a boy." At all events, she carried her point. She had already, under her mother's supervision, acquired proficiency in the usual accomplishments of a girl, music, dancing, drawing, and modern languages, and now she was sent to the public school of Haddington for more solid instruction. Besides Latin, she studied arithmetic and algebra, the latter in company with the boy pupils of the school, who felt for her not only affection but a respect which she is said to have enforced on one occasion by striking with her fist the nose of a boy who had been impertinent, and making it bleed. The master happened to see the gory results of the blow, and demanded who had inflicted it. The boys were all chivalrously silent, and were threatened with a flogging to make them tell. Upon this Jane confessed her guilt, and was punished by relegation to the girls' room. Another story told of her is that, emulating the boys in their difficult feats of strength and agility, she lay down on her face and crawled from one end to the other of a narrow parapet of a bridge at the imminent risk of either breaking her neck or drowning. Exploits of this kind seem to have made her famous in the town, for when, some forty years afterwards, she revisited Haddington, and, too impatient to wait for the sexton to come and unlock the gate of the graveyard, she climbed over the wall, the old man, on finding her inside, and being told how she got in, exclaimed: "Lord's sake, then, there is no end to you!"

Soon after little Jane began to attend the school at Haddington, Irving was appointed its master, and was engaged by Dr. Welsh as private tutor for his daughter. This was the beginning of their acquaintance. It was in 1810, when Jane was nine years old, and Irving, who was born in 1792, was eighteen. Irving's father was a poor tanner in Annan, a town on the shores of the broad Solway, so graphically described by Walter Scott in "Redgauntlet," and from whose swiftly rising tide Irving was once saved while a child, together with his little brother, by an uncle on horseback, very much as Darsie Latimer was saved by his uncle. After the usual preliminary schooling the lad, at the age of thirteen, went to Edinburgh to study at the university, and four years later, in 1809, took his degree. He then entered the Divinity School, and, as was usual for poor Scottish theological students, began teaching for his support while he was pursuing his studies. It was thus, upon the recommendation of his professors, that he obtained the appointment as master of Haddington school.

In person, Irving was very handsome. He was considerably more than six feet in height and powerfully built; his forehead was broad, deep, and expansive; his thick, black, projecting eyebrows overhung dark, small, and rather deep-set penetrating eyes, one of which had an obliquity, the result of long-continued exposure while an infant in the cradle to a light from a side window, but which did not materially detract from his looks; his nose and his mouth were finely shaped, and his whole head nobly cast, and covered with a profusion of black curly hair. It is related of him that when he was preaching at Glasgow, at the age of twenty-seven, he called one day to see a lady who had ordered her maid-servant to tell all visitors she was engaged. The girl broke in upon her in a state of great excitement: "Mem! there's a wonderful grand gentleman called. I couldna say you were engaged to *him*. I think he maun be a Highland chief." "*That* Mr. Irving!" exclaimed another person, "*that* Dr. Chalmers's helper! I took him for a cavalry officer!" A third told Dr. Chalmers himself that Irving looked like a brigand chief. "Well," said Dr. Chalmers, "whatever they say, they never think him like anything but a leader of men."

Irving's strength, courage, and proficiency in athletics were also remarkable. While master of Haddington school he frequently walked with several of his scholars to Edinburgh and back the same evening, a distance of thirty-five miles, to hear Dr. Chalmers preach. At Kirkcaldy, two years later, his feats of swimming were the admiration of the beholders; and when, on a pedestrian excursion with a comrade, some tourists

EDWARD IRVING.

once attempted to exclude the two from the sitting-room of the inn where they had ordered dinner, he calmly threw open the window, and, turning to his companion, said, "Will you toss out or knock down?" This remark, coupled with his powerful appearance and determined expression, immediately procured him his rights. On another occasion he had escorted some ladies to a public meeting, where a bullying official attempted to make them fall back from where they stood. "Be quiet, sir, or I will annihilate you," said Irving, raising in his hand a great stick he carried. The crowd burst into laughter, and Irving's party was not further disturbed. With all this he had great tenderness of heart, and a beautiful story is told of him when he was preaching in London. It was in the open air, and a great crowd surrounded him. A child who had been lost was held up by a person who had found it, and who wanted to know what he should do with it. "Give me the child," said the preacher, and it was passed along to him. He stretched out his arms, and the little waif nestled down upon his shoulder, perfectly happy. He then, with the child in this position, went on with his sermon, weaving into it the familiar narrative of the Saviour's blessing of little children, and at the end restored the lost one to its parents. Witnesses of the incident say that they could never think of it without its bringing tears to their eyes. His pastoral ministrations, both in Glasgow and in London, were marked by the gentlest sympathy with the poor and the suffering, and countless anecdotes are told of his generosity, his courtesy, and his success in winning the hearts of those with whom he came into contact. The poet Procter (Barry Cornwall), who saw much of him in London, pronounced him "the most pure and hopeful spirit surely that Scotland ever produced," and wrote of him:

"If his manner had not been so unassuming I might have felt humble before him. But he was so amiable and simple that we all forgot that we stood in the presence of a giant in stature, with mental courage to do battle with any adversary, and who was always ready to enter into any conflict on behalf of his own peculiar faith.

"I never heard him utter a harsh or uncharitable word. I never heard from him a word or a sentiment which a good man could have wished unsaid. His words were at once gentle and heroic.

"No one who knew him intimately could help loving him."

These physical and moral advantages, joined to that intellectual ability for which afterwards Irving was so distinguished, could not fail to make a profound impression upon the susceptible and romantic girl who became his pupil. Their hours of study were from six to eight in the morning, and in winter, when the young tutor arrived, it was still dark. His charge, scarcely dressed, would be peeping out of her room, and, snatching her up in his arms, Irving would carry her to the door, to name to her the stars still shining in the sky. When her regular lessons were over he would go on and teach her logic. She was soon *dux* in mathematics, became familiar with Virgil, and was carried away by the reading of the Æneid to burn on a funeral pyre her doll, as Dido, dissolving into a flood of tears as she saw the last remnants of it blaze up and vanish. It was the rule that her tutor should leave a daily report in writing of her progress, and whenever the report was bad she was punished. One day, according to Mrs. Oliphant, he paused long before putting his verdict on the paper. The culprit sat at the table, small, downcast, and conscious of failure. Irving lingered remorsefully, wavering between justice and compassion. At last, looking at her pitifully, he said, "Jane, my heart is broken, but I must tell the truth," and down went the dreaded condemnation.

This charming intercourse between the youthful teacher and his precocious pupil lasted two years. Irving was a favorite guest at Dr. Welsh's house, and won the affectionate respect both of him and of his wife. He also made many other friends in the town, among them Gilbert Burns, the poet's brother, and Dr. Stewart of Erskine. But Haddington was a small place, and when, in 1812, the mastership of a newly established academy at Kirkcaldy, eleven miles north of Edinburgh, was offered him, he accepted it, and abandoned his little darling, unconscious of the love which even then had begun to knit their hearts together.

Irving's removal to Kirkcaldy led to two important results. It was there that he became engaged to the young lady whom he ultimately married, and there he met Thomas Carlyle and entered upon the intimacy with him which lasted during the remainder of his life. The parish minister of Kirkcaldy, the Rev. Mr. Martin, had several daughters, the eldest of whom, Isabella, Carlyle says, "was of bouncing, frank, gay manners and talk, studious to be amiable, but never quite satisfactory on the side of *genuineness*. Something of affected you feared always in these fine spirits and smiling discourses, to which, however, you answered with smiles. She was very ill-looking withal; a skin always under blotches and discolorment; muddy gray eyes, which for their part never laughed with the other features; pockmarked, ill-shapen, triangular kind of face, with hollow cheeks and long chin; decidedly unbeautiful as a young woman."

In spite of all this, Carlyle adds, she managed to charm poor Irving, "having perhaps the arena all to herself," and he became engaged to her, little forçseeing the unhappy consequences of his thoughtlessness.

Irving remained at Kirkcaldy seven years. During this period the little girl he had taught at Haddington became a woman. In 1818, when she was seventeen, he met her again in Edinburgh, and then, for the first time, he seems to have discovered the real state of his heart. Mrs. Oliphant says of this meeting, apparently blind to its importance:

"He found her a beautiful and vivacious girl, with an affectionate recollection of her old master, and the young man found a natural charm in her society. I record this only for a most characteristic momentary appearance which he makes in the memory of his pupil. It happened that he, with natural generosity, introduced some of his friends to the same hospitable house. But the generosity of the most liberal stops somewhere. When Irving heard the praises of these same friends falling too warmly from the young lady's lips, he could not conceal a little pique and mortification, which escaped in spite of him. When this little ebullition was over the fair culprit turned to leave the room, but had scarcely passed the door when Irving hurried after her and called, entreating her to return for a moment. When she came back she found the simple-hearted giant standing penitent to make his confession. 'The truth is, I was piqued,' said Irving. 'I have always been accustomed to fancy that I stood highest in your good opinion, and I was jealous to hear you praise another man. I am sorry for what I said just now—that is the truth of it.' It is a fair representation of his prevailing characteristic. He could no more have retained what he felt to be a meanness on his mind unconfessed than he could have persevered in the wrong."

It is incomprehensible how Mrs. Oliphant, a woman, should not have discerned in this burst of jealousy an indication of love; and still more incomprehensible, in the light of facts now known to every one, that she should speak of Irving's meeting with Miss Welsh on this occasion as "a most characteristic momentary appearance which he makes in the memory of his pupil." It was, on the contrary, but the beginning of an intercourse with her which lasted for years, and during which not only did Irving become deeply enamoured of his former pupil, but she, as she frankly confessed to Carlyle seven years afterwards, learned to love him "passionately" in return. He frequently visited her at Haddington, and, as everything goes to show, his visits were those of an accepted suitor. It was just after the meeting in 1818 that Carlyle first heard of her from him, "some casual mention, the loving and reverential tone of which had struck me. Of the father he spoke always as one of the wisest, truest, and most dignified of men, of her as a paragon of gifted young girls, far enough from me both, and objects of distant reverence and unattainable longing at that time!"

The next year, 1819, Dr. Welsh died, leaving to his daughter all his little property, which, with characteristic generosity, she made over to her mother, and the household went on as before. Irving was busy preaching at Glasgow, as assistant to Dr. Chalmers; but he came to Edinburgh whenever he had a holiday, and from there walked out to Haddington. On one of these excursions, in June, 1821, he took Carlyle with him to introduce him as a fit person to superintend Miss Welsh's literary studies, being himself either too much occupied or else not fully competent. Carlyle has left behind him this account of the expedition and its results:

"The visit lasted three or four days, and included Gilbert Burns and other figures, besides the one fair figure most of all important to me. We were often in her mother's house; sat talking with the two for hours almost every evening. The beautiful, bright, and earnest young lady was intent on literature as the highest aim in life, and felt imprisoned in the dull element which yielded her no commerce in that kind, and would not even yield her books to read. I obtained permission to send her at least books from Edinburgh. Book parcels virtually included bits of writing to and from, and thus an acquaintance was begun which had hardly any interruption and no break at all while life lasted. She was often in Edinburgh on visit with her mother to 'Uncle Robert,' in Northumberland Street, to 'old Mrs. Bradfute, in George's Square,' and I had leave to call on these occasions, which I zealously enough, if not too zealously sometimes, in my awkward way, took advantage of. I was not her declared lover, nor could she admit me as such, in my waste and uncertain posture of affairs and prospects; but we were becoming thoroughly acquainted with each other, and her tacit, hidden, but to me visible, friendship for me was the happy island in my otherwise dreary, vacant, and forlorn existence in those years."

Carlyle evidently had as yet got no idea of the state of affairs between Irving and Miss Welsh, being, like all incipient lovers, thoroughly engrossed with his own feelings. The truth was that Irving was negotiating, with great hope of success, for a release from his engagement to Miss Martin, which in both his own and Miss Welsh's view of duty constituted a bar to their marriage. But when, in the following February, he received a call from a Scottish church, London, and it became necessary to have the matter settled, Miss Martin held him to his bond. After a struggle which, to use his own words, had almost "made his faith and principles to totter," he resigned himself to his fate and bade farewell to Miss Welsh in a characteristic letter:

"MY WELL-BELOVED FRIEND AND PUPIL: When I think of you my mind is overspread with the most

THOMAS CARLYLE.

affectionate and tender regard, which I neither know how to name or to describe. One thing I know—it would long ago have taken the form of the most devoted attachment, but for an intervening circumstance, and showed itself and pleaded itself before your heart by a thousand actions from which I must now restrain myself. Heaven grant me its grace to restrain myself; and, forgetting my own enjoyments, may I be enabled to combine into your single self all that duty and plighted faith leave at my disposal. When I am in your company my whole soul would rush to serve you, and my tongue trembles to speak my heart's fulness. But I am enabled to forbear, and have to find other avenues than the natural ones for the overflowing of an affection which would hardly have been able to confine itself within the avenues of nature if they had all been opened. But I feel within me the power to prevail, and at once to satisfy duty to another and affection to you. I stand truly upon ground which seems to shake and give way beneath me, but my help is in Heaven. Bear with thus much, my early charge and my present friend, from one who loves to help and defend you, who would rather die than wrong you or see you wronged. Say that I shall speak no more of the fearful struggle that I am undergoing, and I shall be silent. If you allow me to speak, then I shall reveal to you the features of a virtuous contention, to be crowned, I trust, with a Christian triumph. It is very extraordinary that this weak nature of mine can have two affections, both of so intense a kind, and yet I feel it can. It shall feed the one with faith and duty and chaste affection; the other with paternal and friendly love, no less pure, no less assiduous, no less constant—in return seeking nothing but permission and indulgence.

"I was little comforted by Rousseau's letters, though holding out a most admirable moral; but much comforted and confirmed by the few words which your noble heart dictated the moment before I left you. Oh, persevere, my admirable pupil, in the noble admirations you have taken up. Let affectionateness and manly firmness be the qualities to which you yield your love, and your life shall be honorable; advance your admiration somewhat higher, and it shall be everlastingly happy. Oh! do not forbid me from rising in my communications with one so capable of the loftiest conceptions. Forbid me not to draw you upward to the love and study of your Creator, which is the beginning of wisdom. I have returned Rousseau. Count forever, my dear Jane, upon my last efforts to minister to your happiness, present and everlasting.

"From your faithful friend and servant,
"EDWARD IRVING."

The following June Irving took up his residence in London, and on the second Sunday of July began his labors there. Of his subsequent career, at first brilliant, then eccentric, and finally wildly erratic, ending in a death preceded by something like insanity, it is enough here to say that he rapidly became famous, and for a considerable time preached to crowded audiences of the most distinguished people in London. Then, carried away by a fanciful theory of prophecy, he was led to exalt into utterances of the Holy Ghost the rhapsodies of his more excitable hearers, and to ascribing them to the gift of tongues mentioned in the New Testament. Of course he did not long remain in connection with the Church of Scotland, and he had to form an ecclesiastical organization of his own, fragments of which survive to the present day. At last, worn out by excitement and excessive work, he died in December, 1834, a physical and intellectual wreck, at the early age of forty-two.

The tender relations between Irving and Miss Welsh did not entirely cease with his farewell letter. Even after his marriage, which took place Oct. 13, 1823, he retained for her an affection which made him shrink from meeting her. Mr. Froude, in his biography of Carlyle, tells us that it had been intended that she should pay Irving and his wife a visit in London as soon as they were settled, but Irving begged off. He wrote:

"My dear Isabella has succeeded in healing the wounds of my heart by her unexampled affection and tenderness; but I am hardly in a condition to expose them. My former calmness and piety are returning. I feel growing in grace and holiness, and before another year I shall be worthy in the eye of my own conscience to receive you into my house and under my care, which, till then, I should hardly be."

On her part, Miss Welsh, although Carlyle was urgently pressing his suit, seems not to have dismissed Irving entirely from her memory, and to have indulged a lingering hope that she might yet be united to him. Still, she encouraged Carlyle. As Mr. Froude says: "She had no thought of marrying him, but she was flattered by his attachment. It amused her to see the most remarkable person she had ever met with at her feet. His birth and position seemed to secure her against the possibility of any closer connection between them.

Thus he had a trying time of it. In serious moments she would tell him that their meeting had made an epoch in her history, and had influenced her character and life. When the humor changed, she would ridicule his Annandale accent, turn his passionate expressions to scorn, and when she had toned him down again she would smile once more and enchant him back into illusions. She played with him, frightened him away, drew him back, quarrelled with him, received him back again into favor, as the fancy took her." Once, in the summer of 1823, he imagined that a letter which she wrote him amounted to a promise to become his wife, and she hastened to undeceive him. She said:

"My friend, I love you. I repeat it, though I find the expression a rash one. All the best feelings of my nature are concerned in loving you. But were you my brother I should love you the same. No. Your friend I will be, your truest, most devoted friend, while I breathe the breath of life. But your wife never. Never, not though you were as rich as Crœsus, as honored and renowned as you yet shall be."

At last, in April, 1824, six months after Irving had been married, she consented to a half engagement with Carlyle. He was in Edinburgh busy bringing out his translation of Goethe's "Wilhelm Meister," and she came to the city on a visit to a friend. They met, and, as usual, quarrelled, and on making up the quarrel she promised that as soon as his fortune was made she would share it with him. With this crumb of comfort he went to London to prosecute his literary labors, and there continued his intimacy with Irving, in blissful ignorance of the relations between him and Miss Welsh, as his letters to her, full of details about Irving, show. By the beginning of 1825 he saw his way clear to supporting a wife in the modest style to which he had himself been accustomed to live, and he began to urge upon Miss Welsh the fulfilment of her promise. But she still hesitated. She wrote to him: "In requiring you to better your fortune I had some view to an improvement in my sentiments. I am not sure that they are proper sentiments for a husband. They are proper for a brother, a father, a guardian spirit, but a husband, it seems to me, should be dearer still." At the same time, when Carlyle offered to take her at her word and to release her from her promise, she was unwilling to give him up. She said: "How could I part from the only living soul that understands me! I would marry you to-morrow rather; our parting would need to be brought about by death or some dispensation of Providence. Were you to will it, to part would no longer be bitter. The bitterness would be in thinking you unworthy." And again, a little later, she wrote to him: "I know not how your spirit has gained such a mastery over mine in spite of my pride and stubbornness. But so it is. Though self-willed as a mule with others, I am tractable and submissive towards you. I hearken to your voice as to the dictates of a second conscience, hardly less awful to me than that which nature has implanted in my breast. How comes it, then, that you have this power over me? for it is not the effect of your genius and virtue merely. Sometimes, in my serious moods, I believe it is a charm with which my good angel has fortified my heart against evil."

The relations of the pair might have continued on this footing indefinitely but for the unexpected interference of a well-meaning but imprudent friend of Irving's. This was Mrs. Basil Montague, with whom Irving had become intimate when he went to London to live, in 1823, and to whom he had confided the secret of the attachment between himself and Miss Welsh. Mrs. Montague opened a correspondence both with Miss Welsh and with Carlyle, at first with the ostensible purpose of putting an end to any lingering love which Miss Welsh might feel for Irving, and of reconciling her to a marriage with Carlyle, but finally writing to her a letter dissuading her from the marriage. This letter Miss Welsh at once indignantly enclosed to her suitor, revealing to him, what she had hitherto concealed, how much she had cared for Irving, and throwing herself upon his generosity to forgive her want of candor. His reply was so affectionate and so self-depreciating that it decided her. She went at once to pay his family a visit, and, after many deliberations and changes of plans, during which she once more offered to release him and he to release her, the final arrangements were made. She accepted him bravely as her husband, and they were married on the 17th of October, 1826.

Mr. Froude has been severely censured as painting in too dark colors Carlyle's grim, savage humor, his thoughtless cruelty to his wife, and her unhappiness; but the documentary evidence he has presented fully justifies him. Mrs. Carlyle said herself, not long before her death: "I married for ambition. Carlyle has exceeded all that my wildest hopes ever imagined of him; and I am miserable." Her husband, indeed, appreciated her talents and found pleasure in her society, but he never seems to have experienced for her the passion of love as it is commonly understood. The pair had no children, and, as Mr. Froude tells us, when Carlyle was busy his wife rarely so much as saw him save when she would steal into his dressing-room in the morning while he was shaving. That mutual physical attraction, therefore, which, in spite of all that may be said to the contrary, is essential to complete conjugal union, was wanting to them, and intellectual sympathy could not fill its place. In other respects, too, the couple were uncongenial. She had been the darling of parents in easy circumstances, and had been reared in luxury and accustomed to all the refinements of life. He was the son of a poor stonemason, and his habits were those of a rough Scottish peasant. Hardships which to him were natural and customary were to her torture. After her death, indeed, the truth burst upon him and he was justly overwhelmed with remorse for his conduct. He saw, too late, how cruel he had thoughtlessly been to the delicate flower he had taken into his keeping, and he vainly sought to atone for it by lamentation and self-reproaches.

Irving appears to have met Mrs. Carlyle only four times after her marriage. The first was when she was living at Edinburgh in 1827. His call lasted but half an hour, and at the end of it he insisted, with more zeal than tact, on praying with her and her husband. The next year Carlyle brought him out to spend two or three days at his Craigenputtoch farm, and he seemed cheerful and happy. Again, when the Carlyles went to London on a visit in 1831, Irving came to see them one evening, and Mr. Carlyle, in Mrs. Carlyle's presence, and with her assent, essayed to extricate him from the delusions into which he had fallen. Her feelings may be guessed from what she afterwards said: "There would have been no tongues had Irving married me." In 1834, the first year of her permanent residence in London, and the last of Irving's life, he called on her at her house in Cheyne Row, and staid about twenty minutes. "Ah, yes," he said to her, looking round the room, "you are like an Eve; make every place you live in beautiful." In less than two months afterwards he died.

Whether Mrs. Carlyle would have been happier with Irving for a husband instead of Carlyle is doubtful. That Irving would have been to her most tender, loving, and married, not from love, but from a sense of duty, compels us to believe; but whether his failure in his career, and the want of that gratification of her pride and satisfaction of her ambition which she got with Carlyle, would not have been as sore a trial to her as Carlyle's harshness is not so sure. Irving, like Carlyle, was a man of genius, but his genius was confined within the narrow limits of religious enthusiasm, and he had little or no sympathy for anything that lay outside. He was even alarmed when Carlyle on undertaking Miss Welsh's literary education in 1821, began to teach her German, and to open to her the treasures of German literature. He feared, as he wrote to Carlyle, that she would escape altogether out of the region of his sympathies. The development of their respective minds could, therefore, scarcely have failed to result in a radical disagreement, so that she would have been, in a different way, as unhappy with him as she was with Carlyle, without the compensation that Carlyle's talents and fame afforded

www.ingramcontent.com/pod-product-compliance
Lightning Source LLC
Chambersburg PA
CBHW031740230426
43669CB00007B/418